# SPIRAL OF THE THREE MOTHERS

*An Aboriginal Wisdom*
*Guide to the High Holydays*

## GERSHON WINKLER,
## MIRIAM MARON

**BALBOA.**PRESS
A DIVISION OF HAY HOUSE

Balboa Press books may be ordered through booksellers or by contacting:

Balboa Press
A Division of Hay House
1663 Liberty Drive
Bloomington, IN 47403
www.balboapress.com
844-682-1282

Because of the dynamic nature of the Internet, any web addresses or links contained in this book may have changed since publication and may no longer be valid. The views expressed in this work are solely those of the author and do not necessarily reflect the views of the publisher, and the publisher hereby disclaims any responsibility for them.

The author of this book does not dispense medical advice or prescribe the use of any technique as a form of treatment for physical, emotional, or medical problems without the advice of a physician, either directly or indirectly. The intent of the author is only to offer information of a general nature to help you in your quest for emotional and spiritual well-being. In the event you use any of the information in this book for yourself, which is your constitutional right, the author and the publisher assume no responsibility for your actions.

Any people depicted in stock imagery provided by Getty Images are models, and such images are being used for illustrative purposes only. Certain stock imagery © Getty Images.

Print information available on the last page.

ISBN: 978-1-9822-7751-2 (sc)
ISBN: 978-1-9822-7752-9 (e)

Balboa Press rev. date: 11/16/2021

We dedicate this book to

**Jack and Sue Witkin**

Whose support through the years has enabled us to study and to share the lesser-promulgated wisdom of our people's ancient traditions

# Table of Contents

# Spiral of the Three Mothers

> Three Mothers: Wind, Water, and Fire. And they are a great and wondrous mystery veiled within the unknowable by six seals, and out of them were born the Fathers. Mother Fire created Sky, Mother Water created Earth, and Mother Wind maintains balance between them.[1]

Right now, as you are reading these words, you are being spiraled into being and becoming, compliments of what our ancient mystics called שָׁלֹשׁ אִמּוֹת (*sha'losh ee'moth*) the Three Mothers of Creation, namely -- מַיִם אֵשׁ רוּחַ (*ru'ah, aish, ma'yim*) -- Wind, Fire and Water. Wind conceived of the Creator's intent and birthed Wisdom, Fire conceived of Creator's intent and birthed Light, Water conceived of Creator's intent and birthed Darkness.[2]

The Three Mothers are the Conjures of Creation. They are called "Mothers" because they draw from the primeval intent of Creator, like womb draws from seed, awakening the purpose therein. Each of the Three Mothers is a primary carrier of one of the three phases of process, of Creation – Thought, Resonance, and Manifestation. The Three Mothers are represented

---

[1] *Sefer Yetzirah* 3:2
[2] *Midrash Shemo't Rabbah* 15:22

in the sacred Hebrew runes א מ שׁ which in turn represent the spiraling of Thought into Resonance into Manifestation, or מַחְשָׁבָה דִּבּוּר מַעֲשֶׂה (*mah'shavah, dee'bur, ma'aseh*).

The rune א is the primary carrier of the unfolding of Thought; מ is the primary carrier of the unfolding of Resonance, and שׁ is the primary carrier of the unfolding of Manifestation. All three qualities are turning and churning within each of the Three Mother conjurers, but each is a **primary** Keeper of one of these attributes. א is the Keeper of Air – *a'veer* אֲוִיר -- or Wind – *ru'ah* רוּחַ; מ is the Keeper of Water – *ma'yeem* מַיִם; and שׁ is the Keeper of Fire – *aish* אֵשׁ.

The first speck of Creation begins then with Mother א, emerging from the primordial thought of the unknowable, un-name-able One by Whose Will all came into being, by whose Intent all continues to exist and to become. This is First Breath, First Wind, imploding from out of First Thought. Eventually, it became also the first symbol, or letter, of the Hebrew alphabet: א. And we called it *"A'luf,"* which means "Chief." All the runes in the Hebraic system double as numbers as well. The numerical representation of א is 1. As Chief, א encompasses the qualities of the remaining two mothers, Water and Fire, as air retains moisture and warmth, respectively. Its pronunciation is silent; it is Thought.

The second Mother is מ, pronounced *"Mem."* The מ represents Womb and is in fact shaped like one. It is here where First Seed moves from the Realm of Thought into the realm of Resonance, from the world of Absence into the world of Presence. Absence implies that there is something but it is not yet revealed. It is, after all, Thought. It is but isn't. In the womb of מ, what was Thought begins to take on form, substance. In מ, Thought begins to reverberate. It begins to speak, to express itself, which in Hebrew is the same exact word for Resonate: דבּור (*dee'bur*). It speaks the thought into becoming; it welcomes the seed of Divine Intent to open and become present in the abyss of absence. Eventually, it became the symbol in our tradition representing the number 40, associated with the weeks of gestation in pregnancy. As womb, מ is pronounced with the mouth closed, as in *mmmmm*. Think before you speak and you will prevent a premature birth.

The third Mother is ש, pronounced "Sheen," which is Hebrew for "Transformation." It is three-pronged, for it calls into Action all three attributes of all three Mothers, Thought, Resonance and Action. The phases of Transformation involves the three-part process of Choice (thought) spiraling into

Resonance --meaning that the decision you make begins to resonate throughout your being, sending shivers up and down your spine -- and Action, acting on it, taking the first step in the direction of the choice, in the direction of manifesting that primal thought and actually making it happen. Eventually, שׁ became the symbol for the number 300. It is pronounced the way a crackling fire sounds: *shhhhhh*.

The Hebraic word for **Wind** – רוּחַ (*ru'ah*) -- also means Spirit, Air, Atmosphere, and Breath. In other words, רוּחַ is the unseeable, untouchable mystery we might refer to as "Life-Force." It is in other words the Life-Force **beyond** us, the Life-Force **around** us, and our act of inhaling and exhaling both, which in turn perpetuates the Life-Force with**in** us. In very old versions of this wisdom, this word implies "air." And not incidentally is the opening rune for this word what later became the Hebrew letter ר (*raysh*), which means "root," implying the exact same underlying meaning as the "Chief" of א, as Chief is the root of the clan or tribe.

All of these manifestations of Wind, of רוּחַ, are infused with **Wisdom**, meaning they carry the wisdom of Creator's intent for Creation to become.

The Hebraic word for **Fire** -- אֵשׁ (*aish*) -- is rooted in the word -- אוּשׁ (*ush*) -- which implies

8

"Confirmed," or "Strong," or "To Exist." Fire lives in the heart. It is burning fiercely and fuels our existence. It kindles emotions, whether elation or depression, and everything in between, all of which, as we know, can be quite powerful. Like the dance of flame, our emotions dance constantly between faith and doubt, joy and sorrow, deciding and regretting, high and low. Fire of Heart also illuminates us, bringing us a clarity, an awareness not always awakened by our minds alone, and in that way it births the light within us.

And finally, we have the Hebrew word for **Water** – מַיִם (*mayim*)– which at its root implies Fluidity, as in calming, as in softening what has hardened, soothing what has become inflamed, welcoming what is latent and – like the shape of its letters – enwombing future.

Water thrives through**out** the body, keeping us permeable, nimble and agile. It flows from Above, from beyond us, whether from the sky or from the faucet, as water flows downward, seeping everywhere and filling any space not already occupied.

The Wisdom of Wind harmonizes the upper and lower realms, mediates between the Realm of Water, flowing from above, and the Realm of Fire, imploding from below.

Fire of Heart is so fierce that were it not for Wind, it would consume the entire body. It is no wonder, then, that there are a number of passageways and vents between the heart (place of fire) and the lungs (place of wind), which enables Wind to foster the Fire of Heart while also controlling its overpowering tendencies and maintaining thereby a proper balance.[3]

Water is about Consciousness. It is therefore dark. No one but you knows what streams through your consciousness moment to moment, sometimes like a gentle babbling brook, sometimes like raging rapids. It awakens the consciousness of body and mind. Without it, our consciousness becomes weakened, our awareness subsides.

**"And from out of the Three Mothers were born the fathers."** What are "the fathers" and why are they not numbered, as in how many of **them** emerged? *Because they ain't **daddies** in the literal sense.* They represent the innumerable ways in which the masculine energies emerging from the Three Mothers of Creation apply finishing touches to their creations, respectively. In other words, while it is the feminine force which enwombs and cultivates Creator's intent, it is the masculine force which

---

[3] *Sefer Ha'Zohar*, Vol. 4, folio 227b

applies the identifying **outer** expressions of that intent, of what the feminine has birthed. Having done so, the fathers then package their finishing touches, their creation of outward definitions, within what we mortals call "seeds," and then leave it to the feminine Earth to enwomb them and bring their "program" to fruition. The feminine attribute of Earth is referred to in our mystical tradition as אֵמָא תַּתָּאָה (ey'ma thatha'a), or "Mother of the Below Realm," also known as "sister" and "friend." Later we will be learning of עִלָּאָה אֵמָא (ey'ma ee'la'a) Mother of the **Above** Realm, and how the two unite on the festival of Yom Kippur in intimate embrace, symbolic of the kiss of heaven and earth, of the energies of Creator and the responding energies of Creation.

The third-century Rabbi Huna taught that עָפָר זָכָר, אֲדָמָה נְקֵבָה, dry soil – עָפָר (afar) -- is masculine, and wet clay – אֲדָמָה (adamah) -- is feminine. "And Creator brought together dry soil, male, and wet clay, female, in order that the vessels become solidified.[4] As is written: "וַיִּיצֶר יהוה אֱלֹהִים אֶת הָאָדָם עָפָר מִן הָאֲדָמָה -- And *Elo'heem* formed The Adam; soil from the clay"[5] -- dry from wet. This is very much like the Creation of

---

[4] *Midrash Bereisheet Rabbah* 14: הַיּוֹצֵר הַזֶּה מֵבִיא עָפָר זָכָר וְאֲדָמָה נְקֵבָה כְּדֵי שֶׁיִּהְיוּ כֵּלָיו בְּרִיאִין

[5] Genesis 2:7

Earth, as is written: וַיֹּאמֶר אֱלֹהִים: יִקָּווּ הַמַּיִם מִתַּחַת הַשָּׁמַיִם אֶל מָקוֹם אֶחָד וְתֵרָאֶה הַיַּבָּשָׁה -- "And *Elo'heem* said: 'Let the waters beneath the Heavens gather to one side so that the Dry will become revealed."[6] In other words, God created First Human dry from wet, Soil from Clay, just like our ancestors would make their pottery, first shaping the wet clay accordingly, and then coating the clay with dry earth to solidify what has been shaped. In this way, wrote the 16ᵗʰ-century Rabbi Yehudah Loew of Prague, "Man is צוּרָה (*tsurah*) and Woman is חוֹמֶר (*ho'mer*)[7] -- צוּרָה representing the external sand that forms around the clay to solidify its shape, חוֹמֶר representing the **internal** clay which comprises the essence, the עֶצֶם (*etzem*) of the substance. The feminine creates the new while the masculine applies the finishing touches.

So while Mother-Water, for instance, created the **essence** of water, its characteristics and qualities, the Fathers who **emerged** from Mother-Water formed water's visible outer layer and texture. The same with Fire and Wind. What Fire and Wind are in their essence, in their mystery, were conjured out of Creator's intent by the feminine forces, the so-called "Daughter of the Tribal Chief," as is written: "All of

---

[6] Genesis 1:9
[7] MaHaRaL in *Chidushei Aggadot*, Vol. 1, folio 136

the Glory of the Daughter of the Tribal Chief[8] is with*in* her,"[9] meaning that the feminine creates **in**ternally, while the masculine is all about the **ex**ternal. The Mothers conceive the essence and mystery of things and the little daddies whom they birthed add particular colors, shapes, and textures to them.

Without the Three Mothers, nothing lives. They carry the Life Force to you and within you by way of every *breath* (Wind). They manifest their energies in the *moisture* of your breath (Water) and in the *warmth* of your breath (Fire). They continuously weave and spiral Creator's intent for Creation to be and become, permeating every aspect of the corporeal. They make their home in the sacred smoke – in עָשָׁן (*Ashan*), the Hebrew word for "Smoke" and acronym for *O'lam, Shanah, Nefesh* -- נֶפֶשׁ שָׁנָה עוֹלָם – Universe, Year, and Embodiment, or

---

[8] מֶלֶךְ *Melekh* in Hebrew, always translated as "King," although there was no such animal as "King" in the days when those words were written over 3,000 years ago. The concept of "King," wrote Martin Buber, came much later as the clans of early humanity began to gradually politicize the leadership of their tribal deities (Martin Buber: *On the Bible – Eighteen Studies* [ed. N. Glatzer], p. 66). Translations of our ancient writ sadly reflect more the lingo of medieval Europe than of Ancient Israel. מֶלֶךְ is an ancient Hebrew word for "Clan Chief," or "Arbitrator."

[9] Psalms 45:14

Space, Time, and Matter. And we celebrate them during the three cycles of our harvest season, or what we might call the three "Mother's Days" -- Mother Wind on Rosh Hashanah, Mother Fire on Yom Kippur, and Mother Water on Sukkot.

# ROSH HASHANAH

## Wind of the Day

**Mother Wind breezes in most prominently on Rosh Hashanah,** as wind implies shifting, changing, transformation, renewal, all the themes of Rosh Hashanah, and, of course, the sounding of the Ram's Horn which involves a great deal of wind. In the Creation Story, Adam and Eve, still chewing on the Forbidden Fruit, are described as hearing the Voice of Creator strolling in the Garden "to the Wind of the Day."[10] While it is Creator who **enables** the Wind, it is Creation which **channels** it and directs it. Thus, did the 2nd-century Rabbi Akiva teach that whether or not everything is predestined, the choice nevertheless remains ours.[11] This **choice** -- how we choose to direct the actions of our embodiment of the Wind within us – of course varies from day to day, year to year, or from circumstance to circumstance, and is therefore referred to in the Torah as "Wind of the Day" as in "which way is the wind blowing today?" -- meaning,

---

10 Genesis 3:8
11 *Mishnah, Avot* 3:19

15

what kinds of choices were made today, and what sorts of consequences have they wrought? Like the ancient rabbis put it: "Each day has its own dilemmas,"[12] its own fresh translation of the God Breath which is calling Creation into becoming. This is why it is called "Wind of the **Day**," as opposed to "Wind of **God**." In other words, what began as אֱלֹהִים רוּחַ (*ru'ah elo'heem*) -- Wind/Spirit of God -- hovering over the primal waters of Genesis, is now reflecting back as (*ru'ah ha'yom*), Wind/Spirit of the Day, of the Situation or of the Circumstance as it developed from out of Creation's responses, Creation's choices and the resulting drama. When the Torah then describes Creator as moving through the Garden of Eden "toward the Wind of the Day," the scenario is such that Creator is maintaining its enabling of the Otherness of Creation, exploring, so to speak, where things happen to be at, what choices have been acted-on during that particular day, and what unique circumstances have resulted.

The question posed to First Human after they ate of the Forbidden Fruit was then not "What have you **done**?" but more to the core "Where are you **at**?" -- as in what choices did you make **today** in regard to your embodiment of my Wind, of my enabling your existence as a separate and unique Other? Creator's concern is staying connected with Creation.

---

[12] *Talmud Bav'li, Berachot* 9b

The artist does not seek to **abandon** his work. He may let **go** of it, but he will **wonder** about it, what it has meant to others, and how did they choose to interpret it. And so, the verse in the Torah makes all the more sense when it says: "And they heard the sound of *Elo'heem* moving through the Garden to the Wind of the Day," as in Creator traversing its infinite Self and its ideals of absoluteness to meet Creation in tempo with the rhythm of its Otherness and the finite reality of relativity in which it flourishes. This is the underlying theme of Rosh Hashanah: (*ha'yom harat o'lam*) -- "Today the world is conceived."[13] We chant these words following each series of wind blasts from the *Shofar*, for the Wind of Time is conceived anew on this very day.

---

[13] Rosh Hashanah Liturgy

# Days of Awe? Or Awesome Days?

Contrary to what most people assume, Rosh Hashanah and Yom Kippur are not about trembling in the face of future uncertainty with fear, but rather dancing in the face of future uncertainty with **faith**. These important festivals are intended to remind us to believe in ourselves and in each other, a task that is ironically far more challenging than that of believing in God. Nor are these holydays about feeling guilty or atoning for sins, as most people assume. "The worst sin," taught the eighteenth-century Rabbi Yisro'el Ba'al Shem Tov, "is letting yourself believe that you're a sinner." While Yom Kippur, for instance, is described in the Hebrew Scriptures as a "Day of Atonement," the atonement itself occurs by way of celebrating, not brooding. Therefore, the ancient rabbis describe the Yom Kippur of antiquity as by far "the most **festive** holy day in Israel."[14] It was a day of fasting and introspection -- yes -- and it was also a day of celebration and dance, as we will demonstrate later. The prophets of old reminded our ancestors how the so-called Days of Awe actually have no room for somberness and were to be commemorated with gladness of heart and festive celebrations:

---

[14] *Talmud Yerushalmi, Ta'anit* 23a

וַיֹּאמֶר נְחֶמְיָה וְעֶזְרָא וְה_לְוִיִּם הַמְּבִינִים אֶת־הָעָם לְכָל־הָעָם: הַיּוֹם
קָדֹשׁ־הוּא לַיהוָה אֱלֹהֵיכֶם אַל־תִּתְאַבְּלוּ וְאַל־תִּבְכּוּ כִּי בוֹכִים כָּל־
הָעָם כְּשָׁמְעָם אֶת־דִּבְרֵי הַתּוֹרָה:

*And Nehemiah along with Ezra and the Levites were explaining the festival to the people when they noticed how solemnity had set in among the masses. And they said to all the people, "This day is holy to Hawayah your God: do not grieve or weep," for all the people were weeping as they listened to the words of the Teaching.*

וַיֹּאמֶר לָהֶם לְכוּ אִכְלוּ מַשְׁמַנִּים וּשְׁתוּ מַמְתַקִּים וְשִׁלְחוּ מָנוֹת
לְאֵין נָכוֹן לוֹ כִּי־קָדוֹשׁ הַיּוֹם לַאֲדֹנֵינוּ וְאַל־תֵּעָצֵבוּ כִּי־חֶדְוַת יְהוָה
הִיא מָעֻזְּכֶם:

*[Nehemiah] further said to them, "Go, eat schmaltzy foods and drink sweet beverages and send portions of your meals to whoever has not prepared their own meal, for the day is holy to our Cosmic Master. Do not be sad, for the very act of your rejoicing in Hawayah is in it**self** the very source of your empowerment."*

וְהַלְוִיִּם מַחְשִׁים לְכָל־הָעָם לֵאמֹר הַסּוּ כִּי הַיּוֹם קָדֹשׁ וְאַל־תֵּעָצֵבוּ:

*And the Levites went about calming the people, saying, "Hush! for the day is holy; do not be sad."*

וַיֵּלְכוּ כָל־הָעָם לֶאֱכֹל וְלִשְׁתּוֹת וּלְשַׁלַּח מָנוֹת וְלַעֲשׂוֹת שִׂמְחָה גְדוֹלָה
כִּי הֵבִינוּ בַּדְּבָרִים אֲשֶׁר הוֹדִיעוּ לָהֶם:

*And all of the people went to their homes to eat and to
drink and to deliver portions of their meals to others,
and to make great merriment, for they understood the
things in which they had been taught.*[15]

Why do we don white on the Days of Awe? --
the rabbis asked more than two thousand years ago --
because they are not only Days of *Awe* but more
importantly Days of Faith and Rejoicing, faith in
Creator erasing away our wrongs as a cloud dissipating
in the wind.[16] They were speaking of wrongs committed
within ourselves, and between ourselves and Creator.
Wrongs committed toward others, however, continue
to linger like a stubborn San Francisco fog until we
work it out with the one(s) we've wronged. And if the
other party refuses our attempts to heal the rift, the
Torah tells us not to take the failure thereof upon
ourselves.[17]

Both holidays, then, are linked to the celebration
of possibility, new beginnings, and remind us that
opportunities for fresh starts don't occur once a year
but come to us in every moment through**out** the year.

---

[15] Nehemiah 8:9-11

[16] *Talmud Yerushalmi, Rosh Hashanah* 7a; based on Isaiah 44:22

[17] Leviticus 19:17

Both holidays challenge us to do what the trees begin to do during the season in which these festivals occur: release old growth to make room for new budding. Both holidays challenge us to harvest our inner fields in the season when we harvest our outer fields; to glean what is right and truth within us and discard what is wrong and false within us. They are basically festivals of spiritual composting, mulching and recycling.

The term "Rosh Hashanah," by the way appears only once in the entire body of the ancient Hebrew Scriptures, and not as a festival that today bears its name but as an umbrella term inclusive also of Yom Kippur, as is written in Ezekiel 40:1 – בְּעֶשְׂרִים וְחָמֵשׁ שָׁנָה לְגָלוּתֵנוּ בְּרֹאשׁ הַשָּׁנָה בֶּעָשׂוֹר לַחֹדֶשׁ -- "In the twenty-fifth year of our exile [to Babylon], on Rosh Hashanah, in the Tenth Day of the Month...." The 10th day of the month of the Hebrew New Year cycle – the Moon of תִּשְׁרֵי (Tish'rey) -- happens to be Yom Kippur.[18]

רֹאשׁ הַשָּׁנָה Rosh Hashanah does not in any way translate as "New Year." Literally, it means "Beginning of Transformation." רֹאשׁ (rosh) means "Head of, or "Root of," and שָׁנָה (shanah) literally translates as "year" in Hebrew but at its root connotes

---

[18] Leviticus 23:27

"transformation," and indeed as autumn approaches so does the challenge of personal and communal transformation. Outside, the colors of the leaves are beginning to change, as is the temperature, and the aroma in the air. The twelfth-century Kabbalist Rabbi Avraham ben Dovid taught: "As arrangements of the stars shift, so does the nature of our earth, through the changing of the seasons. And, in turn, changes in the seasons of our earth creates changes in the soul of every living being."[19]

Seasonal changes, Judaism teaches, are not phenomena confined to what goes on outside of us in what we refer to as Nature, but they affect us just as dramatically deep **in**side us. The purpose of the High Holyday services, then, are not to torture congregants with hours of prayer but to help them midwife new paradigms in their lives, spiritual, physical, emotional and otherwise; to help coach the birthing of something magically new and refreshingly alive in the year to come.

We should therefore not perceive the High Holydays as "Days of Awe" but as "Awesome Days," the onset of an extended cycle of ceremonies and celebrations that move us through the very

---

[19] Commentary on *Sefer Yetsirah* 3:4

transformation that is taking place in our earth. The paradigm is changing. This is an opportunity to move with it. We live in exciting times. Let's welcome them without trepidation and a great deal of *chutzpah* and joy, something we desperately need in these times.

# Without the Peel, Please

But is it really a **New** Year? Pray tell, what has ever been so "new" at the shift of all annual cycles? Wasn't it wise old Solomon who said that whatever will **be** already **was**? And that whatever we suppose is new is little more than old hat?[20]

If you think about it, the only thing "new" is what we've invented, what we've created external to our organic Selves, but little about us has really changed significantly enough to warrant the title "New." There were nice people like you in ancient times as well. There were liberal-minded folks thousands of years ago too. Jewish women wore *tallis* and *tefillin*[21] and were called up to the *bimah* to read from the Torah back then too.[22] There were wars and genocides back then too. And we can go on and on with infinite examples of how, globally, the overall human condition hasn't changed much at all – for better or for worse - in spite of the thousands of New Years, Jewish or otherwise, that have come and gone.

---

[20] Ecclesiastes 1:9

[21] *Talmud Bav'li, Eruvin* 96a

[22] *Talmud Bav'li, Megilah* 23a

So why bother with all the hustle and bustle of "New Year"?

Well, for one thing, nowhere in the entire Torah is there any mention of *Rosh Hashanah*, nor any hint to the **concept** of "New Year." Rather, what we today call Rosh Hashanah is referred to in the Torah as "Festival of the Ingathering in the Going Out of the Year."[23] Gathering-in while going out, or dancing while sitting still, or leaping up while lying down. Elsewhere, Rosh Hashanah is referred to as תְּרוּעָה זִכְרוֹן (*zikhron teru'ah*), literally "Memory of the Sounding."[24] Memory of **what** sounding? The primal sounding of Beginning;[25] the First Sound of Genesis, of the Dream of Creator imploding into realization; the first sound of a newborn emerging from out of the womb; the sound of what is **yet** to be, freeing itself from what **used** to be -- all of which we incorporate within the sound of the ritual Ram's Horn, or שׁוֹפָר (*sho'far*).

The sound we are to remember is also the song of the Three Mothers spiraling through the spiraling shape of the Shofar. The song of Mother Wind in the long *even* blast, the song of Mother Fire in the *three-part* blast, representative of the three parts of flame

---

[23] Exodus 23:16
[24] Leviticus 23:24
[25] *Talmud Bav'li, Rosh Hashanah* 27a

(blue, orange, white), and song of Mother Water sounded in the *multiple successive* blasts, mimicking the sound of rain drops.

> With the approach of the New Year, we blow our breath through the ram's horn [*shofar*], to unify the elements of Fire, Wind, and Water, to bring them into a single voice that is the song of Earth. Through this sound we awaken the Voice of the Above so that the song of Heaven joins in unison with the song of Earth until they become one unified resonance that shatters and confuses all the forces of divisiveness.[26]

What we call "New Year" or "Head of the Year," then, or "Beginning of the Year" or any other variant of translation accorded the term *Rosh Hashanah* has therefore little to do with the year to come. Rather, it is a period of "gathering **in** while letting **go**." This means bringing in the yield of past (*a la* "memory") while letting go of the Theater of Time Unfolding. Because it is Time which moves us to and through our life circumstances, in and out of encounters both welcome and unwelcome. "Time," wrote Abraham Joshua Heschel, "is a circle whose center is everywhere and whose periphery is nowhere."[27] On Rosh Hashanah we gather-in the yield, the gifts of what **was** in the **previous** year, while letting go of the year itself,

---

[26] *Sefer Ha'Zohar*, Vol. 4, folio 99b
[27] *Moral Grandeur and Spiritual Audacity*, p. 17

releasing the dramas out of which those gifts had unfolded. In other words, there is no "New" year if we're still hanging on to the "Old" year.

"Day of **the** Remembering" then means the task of choosing the memories that can best catapult you into something **genuinely** new. But for those memories -- those yields of yesteryear -- to become potent enough for such a powerful launch into tomorrow, they must be divested of their peels, the layers of trauma and pain that would otherwise dull their efficacy to inspire renewal, to give voice to that within you which waits to be birthed.

Rosh Hashanah then challenges us to celebrate the gift that is the restoration of our ancient homeland without the trauma that led to 1948 looming in the background. Or to celebrate the love you have in your life without the series of unfortunate events which led up to you meeting them looming in the background. Or to celebrate your recovery from whatever, without the endless doctor visits, grueling tests and surgeries you went through looming in the background.

In this way, *Rosh Hashanah* becomes what it really means in literal translation: "Beginning of the Transformation," as it opens up the obscure doorway to *Yom Kippur*, to forgiveness of self and of other, and becomes thereby a journey of healing, which is what renewal is all about. It is then no wonder that the ancient prophet Ezekiel considered *Yom Kippur* too as an integral part of *Rosh Hashanah*. It was in fact he who originally gave the holiday its name, as mentioned above.[28] For he understood that the delight which awaits within the fruition of our past can only become revealed to us when we peel it first.

---

[28] Ezekiel 40:1

# Creating Human

> Taught Rabbi Eliezer (1st century): In the first hour of Rosh Hashanah is when the idea arose in God's mind to create the human to begin with. In the second hour, he ran it by the angels. In the third hour, he gathered together some clay. In the fourth hour, he compressed the clay. In the fifth hour, he shaped it. In the sixth hour, he erected it. In the seventh hour, he cast the Soul of Life into it. In the eighth hour, he placed the newly-formed human in the Garden. In the ninth hour, he instructed the human. In the tenth hour, the human disobeyed the instruction. In the eleventh hour, the human was judged. In the twelfth hour, the human was pardoned, and left the Garden.[29]

At core, you are a specific idea that arose in the mind of Creator, a concept that is unique to all other concepts. Creator then took the idea of you and ran it by the angels. Angels are beings who both embody and manifest Divine Intent. They are the translators of Creator's ideas. And so you had to be proposed to them at a celestial board meeting to determine whether you were actually do-able. Once approved, Creator gathered some earth specifically designated for what you would be all about. So, maybe some fertile soil

---

[29] *Midrash Pesikta D'Rav Kahane* 23:1

from Norway, a few sprinkles of sand from the Sub-Saharan, a chunk of fresh clay from the Himalayans, and a little chip off an Alaskan iceberg. (Now you know why you went on that Norwegian cruise, dreamed of visiting Morocco, made frequent visits to Tibet, and bought a summer place in Alaska.) Remember -- you were created from the Four Directions, or what in our tradition we call the Four Winds, as well as from earth gathered from all regions of the planet.[30]

Next, Creator lovingly tapped the various sprinklings of earth chosen for your composite, packing it tight and firming it up so that it might be ready for shaping. Then, when the idea of you had taken shape, you were activated, plugged in, imbued with the Life Breath to become the living creature that you are. At this point, you were placed in a particular life situation that would be the most fertile arena for your evolution, your personal "Garden." Next, you were given instructions on how to negotiate the bends, curves, and bumps in this arena, but of course you had ideas of your own which went against your "better judgment" and ended up amid a barrage of consequences out of which you emerged – or will eventually emerge -- more liberated than you could ever have imagined possible. In other words, the very bleakness with which you presumed you'd been

---

[30] *Sefer Ha'Zohar*, Vol. 1, folio 130b, and Vol. 2, folios 13a and 23b

stricken became -- or is yet to become -- the catalyst for a birthing of a You that is unparalleled.

Rosh Hashanah is then about how First Human lives within each of us in that each of us is a First Human in our own right, there never ever having been anyone remotely like any of us on the face of the earth. Each of us is an original, the 18th-century Rebbe Nachmon of Breslav reminded us, a brand new creation; a First Human; an ancestor, a "limited edition." This is a very deep and important aspect of the holiday that too often gets lost amid pages and pages of well-intentioned supplications and exaltations cantorized in the hours-long services at our temples and synagogues.

# "The Human is a Tree"[31]

According to our people's ancient Creation story, First Man and First Woman rose up from out of the earth a tad less than 5,800 years ago on what we today celebrate as Rosh Hashanah. It was a singular entity at first, a strange one, kind of like those creatures that worm their way out of the earth and are both female and male combined, what we today call hermaphroditic. And that is what our people's creation story tells us: "Male and Female did [God] create them, and called **their** name אָדָם *Adam*."[32] Or, as the ancient sages called to them: פַּרְצוּפָא דוֹ (*do' par'tzufa*) – "two-faced," a woman and a man sharing a single body.[33]

And why were they called אָדָם *Adam*? Because they were fashioned from the soil of אֲדָמָה *Adamah*, of clay,[34] and this was rubbed-in by Creator who reminded them later that "you were taken from out of the soil, and you are soil **itself**."[35]

Yes -- we know. We all come from Lucy, and a couple million years ago. Okay. That's what the

---

[31] Deuteronomy 20:19

[32] Genesis 5:2

[33] *Talmud Bav'li, Berachot* 61a

[34] Genesis 2:7

[35] Genesis 3:19

comeback is whenever we retell this story. And it isn't fair. Every ancient people gets to have their story of how it all started, and no one says *Boo*. Instead, we go *ga-ga* over their tales of humans originating in stardust, or coming from the underworld while questioning every detail about **our** story. When Jews try to tell the **Jewish** story...watch out. Missiles replete with skepticism and critique come flying at them faster than a swarm of Wisconsin mosquitoes in mid-summer. We, it seems, are not entitled to our mythology. We and our stories are judged by a whole other set of standards. "The very negation," wrote Martin Buber, "confirmed the [Torah's] claim upon them; they bore witness to the Book in the very act of denying it."[36]

Anyway, in our story, First Man and First Woman rose up from out of the clay of earth, animated by the breath of Creator, joined together in a single body, around 5,800 years ago exactly, on the day we now refer to as *Rosh Hashanah*, or the first day of the seventh moon-cycle of the Hebrew calendar reckoning. (And hopefully, Hallmark Cards will one day pick up on this and make "Happy Birthday, **Human**" cards for Rosh Hashanah instead of those dreary "Happy New Year" cards.)

---

[36] *On the Bible: Eighteen Studies* [ed. N. Glatzer] p. 2

So, at the turning of the year, we celebrate our *humanness*, our origin in the clay, the woman inside us and the man inside us, as well as both our commonalities and our differences, and why God had to eventually **split** us in two. And by the way, in the Hebrew original it doesn't say "Adam" at the onset, as in some guy named "Adam" futzing about the planet, but הָאָדָם (*ha'adam*) "**The** Adam," as in a singular hermaphroditic creature.

And since it's our birthday, it is no wonder that on Rosh Hashanah God waits for **us** to choose the time, and does not impose it on us. It's **our** birthday. So **we** get to choose. "When the angels inquire of God 'When is Rosh Hashanah? When is Yom Kippur?' The Holy Blessed One says to them: 'You ask this of **me**? Come, let you and I both descend to the earthly courts to find out what **they** have decided,' as is written in Leviticus 23:4: 'These are the festival seasons of *Ado'nai* which conjure the sacred, that you shall declare in their rightful seasons' – that **YOU** shall declare, not God, and not the angels."[37]

Now, in studying the ancient teachings, we are also told that Rosh Hashanah is the birthday of **plants** as well. So we have a little competition going on here. Plants and Humans. Animals we can understand. Both

---

[37] *Midrash Devarim Rabbah* 2:14

humans and animals were created in the same cycle of Genesis, the Sixth so-called Day. But **plants**? Were they not created a few cycles **earlier** than we humans, let alone the animals? What, then, is meant by the teaching in the Talmud that "The first day of the month of *Tish'rey* is also Rosh Hashanah for the **herbs?**"[38]

Then again, the same teaching also includes Rosh Hashanah as the Beginning Time for **Seeding**. Birthday, in other words, is not necessarily a creation of something from scratch, but rather a seeding, a planting of future potential, future renewal of what **was**, of what has **been** and of what will hopefully continue. First Woman and First Man were then not necessarily First **Human** but rather the seeding of yet **another** "First" out of many **earlier** Firsts. And so the Kabbalah tells us that prior to Adam the Man and Adam the Woman (who is later named חַוָּה *Ha'vah* [Eve]), there indeed **did** exist other forms of Human, only not the form in which we manifest as humans in our **current** cycle.

We call this theory שְׁמִטּוֹת *shemito't*.[39] The word שְׁמָטָה *Shemitah*[40] means "detachment," and originally

---

[38] *Mishnah, Rosh Hashanah* 1:1

[39] *Ma'arechet Elokut* on *Talmud Bav'li, Chagigah* 13b; *Tiferet Yisrael* in his intro to Chapter 11 of *Talmud Bav'li, Sanhedrin; Tikunei Zohar*, Chapter 36

[40] Deuteronomy 15:1

applied to the practice of leaving one's field untouched, not working it, every seven years – detaching from our sense of ownership of any part of our earth. The שְׁמִטוֹת *shemito't* theory implied that there existed several lifetimes, so to speak, of our earth, each one detached from the other in that each was a distinct world not connected to the one prior.

Remember. God told First Woman and First Man that they are not only of the earth but *are* earth itself.[41] So yes, we have a lot in common with plants. Like plants, we arose out of the earth from what had been seeded in earlier cycles, and like plants we emerged a singular entity comprised of both qualities: Feminine and Masculine. So Rosh Hashanah is a cyclical festival of rites assigned in our tradition not only for us humans but also for plants and trees.[42]

Our Creation story highlights the unique relationship between the newly-sprouted form in which Human emerged 5,800 years ago, and the plants. We find the clue in the so-called **second** chapter of Genesis. There we are told: "And it was a time before there were any *speaking ones* [ancient Hebrew for "Trees" – שִׂיחַ *see'ach*] upon the earth, and before any grasses had sprouted forth, for God had not yet caused it to rain

---

[41] Genesis 3:19 (see also Genesis 18:24 and Psalms 103:15)

[42] *Mishnah, Rosh Hashanah* 1:1

upon the earth, and there was not yet any human to till the soil, to plant seed, to harvest, to steward the earth."[43]

The *Shemitah* theory interprets this narrative to imply that the humans **before** us who lived in earlier forms of our earth did not have a relationship with the land. They didn't seed, didn't plant. They showed no interest in participating in Creator's venture, and so nothing grew, the earth was untended, uncared for, ignored. And so the earth lacked passion, and no mist arose from her to arouse the sky enough to send down the rains to impregnate her with potential. And so God started a whole new cycle of Creation, of Genesis, and kindled the passion of the earth so that a mist arose from the earth and aroused the sky which then responded with rains to satiate the thirst of the earth.[44]

And it was **then** that we were shaped in the soft wet clay forged by the response of Earth to Sky, and it was then that we rose from the mud and received the breath of life from Creator and became "a living soul,"[45] an embodiment of consciousness born out of the kiss of heaven and earth, and who, like the plant beings, would be firmly rooted in the earth while reaching for the heavens, for the beyond.

---

[43] Genesis 2:5

[44] Zohar, Vol. 1, folios 29b,35a, and 46a-b on Genesis 2:6

[45] Genesis 2:7

And we were told we **are** earth and **from** earth and would return **to** earth, and then were acculturated to become in **service** to the earth, and to watch **over** her and **tend** to her.[46] And we emerged masculine and feminine in a single body to seed improved connectedness between the forces of opposites. And we lived from then on amidst trees that spoke to us, symbolic of the blossoming forth of a whole new kinship between human and plant, a relationship in which we recognized our kinship with all of Creation through the tree. Like the ancient rabbis taught us: "The trees –they communicate with one another and with all creations."[47]

This is the form of human that was born anew 5,800 years ago in our story. That is the quality of our humanness that we celebrate on Rosh Hashanah in the month of *Tish'rey* alongside the plant beings. It is a time to go pray if you wish, but don't forget to save a seat for your neighboring cactus or aloe plant or rose bush or local blade of grass. Or at least sneak a kernel or two into the temple. It is their time as well, a joint birthday, a period when the both of you came into being in a whole other way than ever before.

---

[46] Genesis 2:15

[47] *Midrash Bereisheet Rabbah* 13:2

# *Sho'far* as a Ritual of Disentanglement

About 4,000 years ago, the ancestor of the Hebrews, Abraham, was walking up a very steep mountain with his very puzzled son Isaac. To make a very long story very short, he thought that the Creator of Everything had asked him to un-create his son. And so he was going to return the lad to his maker in a pillar of smoke from atop a mountain called מוֹרִיָּה (*mo'ree'yah*), which translates literally as: "God will Guide."

Now listen carefully. This is the part we don't get no matter how many times we read or listen to this disturbing story.

When Abraham is made to realize that Creator had no intention of having him give back his son, Abraham was already in a "giving back" mode and felt so overwhelmingly grateful that he got to **keep** his son that he wanted even the **more** to give something to Creator in return. Creator, in response, humored Abraham by manifesting "a *'Ram of After,'* seized in entanglement by its horn"[48] so that Abraham would have something to gift back to Creator.

This is important. English translations of our

---

[48] Genesis 22:13

precious Hebrew Torah render this part of the narrative as "he saw a ram 'behind him,' caught in 'the thicket' by its horns." Truth be told, there is no mention in the Hebrew text of a "thicket" of any sort. Literally, it reads: "seized in entanglement by its horn." **Period!** Translators are well-meaning in their attempts to fill-in what they presume are gaps in our ancient writ. In other words, if the ram's horn was caught, it must have been in some kind of "thicket." But in reality, there **was** no thicket. The ram is described in the original Hebrew narrative literally as *"seized by its horns in entanglement."* And the word which is translated as "behind him" (*ahar*) -- actually translates as "after," not "behind him." It makes little sense that "he lifted his eyes and saw a ram **behind** him." No, friends, it was smack in **front** of him, and it appeared from out of nowhere, from the Realm of **After,** implying that it wasn't there prior; it wasn't anywhere **near** there before. It appeared "after," as in from out of the dimension of Time in which the event was occurring. Like the ancient rabbis told us long ago, this ram had been created thousands of years prior at the twilight of Genesis,[49] waiting to be conjured at the precise intersection of the Time and Event for which it was intended. As such, it was indeed "seized in entanglement" and by way of its horns, that part of the

---

[49] *Mishnah, Avot* 5:6

ram that it uses for crashing through the barriers of impossibility.

So, yes, like the Rosh Hashanah liturgy tells us, the sounding of the ram's horn is also related to the ram which Abraham offered in the stead of his son Isaac. But it is far more than a ritual in which we remind God of our willingness to sacrifice. It is a ritual in which we remind ourselves of the horn by which the "Ram of **After**" was seized in entanglement! Else, it would have been more appropriate to call forth the reminder of that event by twirling **ropes** during the service rather than sounding the *sho'far*. After all, is not this monumental event known to us as עֲקֵדַת יִצְחָק "the **binding** of Isaac"? That we rather mark the event with a ram's horn instead of a lasso implies that the central theme of this fundamental Rosh Hashanah ritual is the drama of the "**horn**," in that it was seized in entanglement."

But entangled in **what**? If there was no thicket, in **what** then was the ram's horn seized in entanglement?

Exactly. That is precisely the lesson here, the wisdom, the mystery. In what **are** our horns seized in entanglement? Anything specific? Not really, if you think about it. Because each and every time we manage to **dis**entangle, we awaken as if from out of a dream only to find ourselves still stuck. That in which we presume to be caught is but an image of a particular projection born out of our momentary encounter with a momentary situation. But once we disentangle ourselves from that momentary encounter with that momentary situation, the sense of liberation lingers only long enough for the next episode to come along and remind us that we are still ensnared. This, the translators could not wrap themselves around because they, like the rest of us, are too entangled in that which is in essence inexplicable.

The sacred Sound of *Shofar* is then the unintelligible cry of the soul as echoed through the hollow of the horn, of that which in the story of our ancestor's inner-struggle was "seized in entanglement." Unintelligible indeed, because we cannot speak of that which we cannot fathom. The entire story, highlighted in the rites of the turning of the yearly cycle for our people, is a story of the human struggle to reach what cannot be touched and touch what cannot be felt, and grasp what cannot be seen. And the stage upon which this drama takes place is replete with props that have to do with this very struggle, that of yearning to see and to **be** seen by that which chooses to not reveal itself. He "*saw* the mountain from afar," and he "lifted his eyes and *saw* a ram," and "he named the site '*YHWH sees*,' and so it is referred to this day, as 'through the Mountain where *YHWH* will allow Himself to be *seen.'"*[50] Yes, through the mountain, the seeming obstacle, the thickness of the veil, the very entanglement in which we find ourselves seized, for "the Holy Blessed One conceals Himself within the very obstacle that prevents you from discovering Him."[51]

Abraham is not plunging his knife toward his son; he is rather plunging his knife toward the veil that conceals the God he seeks. While in the eleventh hour his knife did not touch his son, it did nonetheless in that moment rip through the curtain – the פַּרְגּוֹד (*par'gawd*) -- shredding all that pretends to separate God from Humankind. In that moment, he saw that he was seen. It is in this ancient narrative, writes Martin Buber, that "the reciprocity of seeing between God and man is directly revealed to us."[52]

The sound which The Three Mothers help us to spiral through the ram's horn is a prayer, a plea: "Please get me *outta* here! Release me from my entanglement in all that severs our connection, in all that imprisons me in the illusion that this is all there is and ever will be! Free me of my entanglement in the realm of attachment! Grant me the strength of my ancestor who

---

[50] Genesis 22:14
[51] 18th-century Rebbe Nachmon of Breslav in *Likutei MoHaRaN*
[52] *Martin Buber On the Bible*, p. 42

dared to take you up on **your** dare until you showed yourself and enabled him to see you seeing **him**!"

The Ram of *After* does not show up to become disentangled until **after**, as in after we've walked that extra mile and stretched beyond our presumed limitations. The "Ram of After" represents that gift of "alternative" that is revealed to us only "after" **we've** revealed ourselves. *YHWH* shadows you, declared the psalmist.[53] He shows up when **we** show up. He reveals when **we** reveal. But only "after." That was the test of Abraham: "**You** first." A test of faith, of trust, of conviction. Go, he was told. **Where**? "I'll tell you **after** – after you have taken the first step and are on your way." And Abraham went.[54] And so may it be, that in the New Year Cycle we too find the *chutzpah*, the dare, to take each our individual steps into the uncertainty of tomorrow, without the entanglement of the fears and assumptions of yesterday. That is the Way of the *Seer*.

---

[53] Psalms 121:5
[54] Genesis 12:1 and 4; 22:2 and 3

# Inscribe Us in the Book of What?

**Rosh Hashanah** is the daring act of calling forth from within us yet- undefined possibilities and giving them shape in word or in imagery, or –better yet -- in the improvisational theatrics of our life-walk. It is on this very special festival that we are invited to apply our artistic abilities in inscribing our hopes and visions for the new year into the sketchbook we've come to know as the "Book of Life." In other words, when we in our celebration of this festive period ask the Maestro of the Universe to "inscribe us into the Book of Life," what we are actually asking is, that our creative renditions of what we hope our new year would look like be published in the *Journal of Future Outlooks*. It's like an annual art contest and we're all invited to participate, and there are no qualifications, prerequisites or application fees. Just bring your best ideas, your most creative visions, your deepest hopes, and submit them by way of the sacred vibration of the *sho'far*.

You see, the *sho'far* has no individuated voice, because it is the sum total of all of our voices; our cries, our laughter, our moans, our chuckles, our whispers, our shouts. In essence, it brazenly facilitates the transmission of our artistry in the face of every opposing indication, every doubt, every cynical thought. The sound of the *Sho'far*, the ancients taught, "shatters the boundaries,"[55] implodes the impediments that prevent us from at least in the **moment** believing in the veracity of our dreams. And a moment is enough. Because that one solitary moment of being one with your vision, one with your hope, is an inerasable point on the canvas of possibility; it is the Mark of Genesis, out of which can emerge dreams often wilder than you'd imagined.

Standing at the doorstep of Newness is not always as simple as it is cracked up to be. Far easier to just repeat the same old stuff, read the same old prayers in the same old way, and perform the same old rituals as we've always done them. Standing at the doorstep of Newness is usually awkward, because we are more inclined to just remain standing there rather than take that bold step across the threshold. During this sacred time, we find ourselves called to inscribe our hopes, and our commitment to those hopes, onto folios in the Book of Life set aside just for us, after which God will color them in and add some finishing touches. We may stand for hours at the threshold, brush in hand, the clean, blank, costly canvas staring us right in the face with its intimidating emptiness, daring us to apply that very first splotch. Because, who knows what it's gonna

---

[55] *Talmud Bav'li, Berachot* 58b ["shatters half the body," the corporeal boundary of our Soul-Self]

look like? Who knows how it's gonna turn out? That initial splatter of ink, that first move into the unknown, can be the ruin of an otherwise perfect scenario! But that's what art is all about. It is a dance with the unknown, a struggle with the undefined. And Rosh Hashanah is an annual opportunity to apprentice with the Cosmic Artist who reminds us that it's about *going for it* even if it may **not** turn out the way we'd hoped. "Just **do**," says the Merciful One, "and whatever it is you end up doing, it is **pleasing** to Me."[56]

On Rosh Hashanah, may what we've forgotten help us to remember, and what we've let go of become that which holds us up; and may the regrets which constrict us become that which liberates us. And whatever we could not conceive yesterday, may we become pregnant with it today.

---

[56] *Talmud Bav'li, Bechorot* 17a

# Festival of Inconceivable Conception

Speaking of conception and pregnancy being a major theme of Rosh Hashanah, it is interesting that our Torah reading during this period includes the stories of two women who were unable to conceive. As we mentioned earlier, in the liturgy for Rosh Hashanah we repeatedly chant *ha'yom ha'rat o'lam* – "Today is the pregnancy of the universe." Yet, a major theme – again – is the story of two women who could **not** get pregnant.

Both women, Sarah and Hannah, wanted to have children of their own. Sarah eventually gave up on her dream[57] and laughed at the idea when at age 90 she was told it was about to happen.[58] Accordingly, she named her miracle boy יִצְחָק *Yitz'chak* (Isaac) -- Hebrew for "Will Laugh," and then restored her long-gone excitement about having a kid by fully embracing Yitz'chak as her own, making **further** sure he was Number One by going so far as to oust his older paternal brother אֱלִישְׁמָע *Yish'ma'el* (Ishmael) – Hebrew for "God Will Listen" -- whom she felt was the "competition."[59]

---

[57] Genesis 16:2

[58] Genesis 18:12

[59] Genesis 21:10

Hannah, on the other hand, never ceased dreaming, hoping, wishing, pleading until she got **her** miracle boy, whom she named שְׁמוּאֵל *Sh'mu'el* (Samuel) -- Hebrew for "God Listened," or: "His Place is With God." It is an obscure word hard to define, but in naming him, she said: "Because I requested him of Infinite-All."[60] Hannah's sense of the gift of her child was more one of "borrowing," acknowledging that a child is not owned but loaned, for us to wean, guide, and then release.[61] She did not allow her years of longing and passion for a child to climax in possessiveness. And whereas Sarah responded to the miraculous gift of her son by claiming him for the pedigree of her immediate family, Hannah responded to the miraculous gift of **her** son by priming him for the sacred service of the nation.[62] Sarah saw in Isaac his contribution to the lineage of her husband Abraham; Hannah saw in Samuel his contribution to the service of God. Ironically, Isaac ended up being nearly **sacrificed** to God by his father. He survives not as the carrier of the lineage as Sarah had envisioned, but the intermediate, the **father** of that carrier, his son *Ya'akov* (Jacob), thus one generation removed. Samuel, on the other hand, becomes a major shaman,

---

[60] First Samuel 1:20

[61] First Samuel 1:28

[62] First Samuel 1:26-28

prophet and tribal leader of **all** of Israel, and is considered one of the greatest of all of our prophets, in par with two of Israel's greatest shamans: Moses and Aaron.[63]

Two women; their deep-felt yearnings for progeny frustrated by physical limitations. The Sarah part laughs and says "It is wonderful that I just won a Mercedes, but I'm too old to **drive** it!"[64] And the Hannah part weeps and says "I want to get on the road so badly and see the beautiful landscape my God has created, but I don't have a **car**!" One gives up and is nonetheless gifted a child by the supernatural intervention of the Creator of Wombs, and one remains adamant and, too, is gifted a child by the supernatural intervention of the Creator of Wombs. One laughs, one cries, signified by the very notes on the ritual Ram's Horn, or שׁוֹפָר *Sho'far*, where the notes of brokenness, of שְׁבָרִים *she'va'reem*, represent the weeping of Hannah and the notes of תְּרוּעָה *teru'ah* sound like Sarah laughing at the prospect of possibility in the face of the impossible. The *Shofar* blasts awaken **both** reactions in us, faith and doubt, as both are sacred, both have their place in the process of our personal struggles of waxing and waning our way through the thick and thin of our life walk.

---

[63] Psalms 91:6
[64] Genesis 18:12

Rosh Hashanah is not only about bringing in a new yearly cycle. It is as much a bringing in of fresh hope in all that we deemed impossible, and in all that frustrates us to tears. It reminds us that being barren is a limitation of the standard operational procedure of the **Known** Realm, but not of the **Un**known Realm.

Science has the first and middle word, but not the last, and neither does Google. Miracle is not just a hand-out, it is a reminder to us of where our very breath comes from, our capacity to move our fingers, lift an eyebrow, appreciate a sunset, delight in a knish, and to use our God-Gifted faculties and resources not only for our own needs but also for the needs of others. May we not need to be dragged up a mountain and bound to an altar to prove the point that Hannah taught us – that we are all on loan.

It is important to know that in the Hebrew vernacular, *Rosh Hashanah* שֵׁאר הַשָּׁנָה written backwards spells *ha'nashah sh'er* שְׁאֵר הַנָּשָׁה, which translates literally as "the forgetting yet remains." What we have forgotten, what we have let go of to make space for the new, yet remains with us as we venture into the unchartered waters of the next cycle. They become seeds of potential that will sprout fresh remembering. What we have forgotten, in other words, are basically memories that have over time become uprooted, symbolized in the uprooted foliage we apply as shelters during the ensuing festival of Sukkot. "The forgetting that yet remains" becomes the subtle behind-the-scenes catalyst for moving us forward toward a fresh remembrance of our most core self, and of our capacity to conceive and birth in spite of all that stands in the way of our doing so.

Because today is the pregnancy of the universe, meaning that today the universe, which in itself is unable to conceive, is miraculously pregnant with whole new possibilities waiting in the shadows of our doubts and skepticism, our resignations and our hopelessness, daring us to reach for them like Hannah, and embrace them like Sarah; to revel-in for ourselves, and to share them with others. And so, on Rosh Hashanah, we do not read from the Creation story in Genesis. Rather, we read about the miraculous births of the patriarch Isaac son of Sarah and the prophet Samuel son of Hannah, both born of women who couldn't but did anyway.

This explains the otherwise puzzling phrase in the Rosh Hashanah liturgy: "Today is the **pregnancy** of the world" as opposed to, say, "the **birth** of the world." Unlike the other creatures with whom we share our world, the human was not conjured. The earth was essentially "barren" when it came to the human. Face it, we're complicated. The "Hannah" part of Earth wanted it real badly nonetheless, while the "Sarah" part gave up on the idea: what's the point? "What is the Human," she asked, "that you should still be thinking about it and that it still occupies your heart?"[65] And so, Earth brought forth trees, grasses, flowers, plants, animals, birds, fish,[66] but she could not birth the human. The **Hannah** of the earth felt a great void in the absence of the human -- "And no trees grew and no grass sprouted because the human was not upon the earth to tend her"[67] -- while the **Sarah** of earth felt that the mist rising from the earth herself was enough to serve the *needs* of the earth -- "And a mist arose from the earth."[68] Hannah, on the other hand, longed for the opportunity to **participate** in bringing forth a being who would steward the earth and appreciate both Creator and Creation: "Grant your handmaiden with the seed of humanity," she prayed, "so that I might in turn gift the manifestation thereof unto Infinite-All."[69]

Creator then personally midwifed the birth of the human in partnership with the earth: "And *Elo'heem* said, 'Let us [**both**] make the human jointly,

---

65 Psalms 8:5 and Job 7:17
66 Genesis 1:11-12, 20 and 24
67 Genesis 2:5
68 Genesis 2:6
69 First Samuel 1:11

in our image and in our likeness,'[70] and *Elo'heem* fashioned the human, dust from out of the clay and blew into its nostrils the Breath of Lives."[71] Created are we in the image of those two qualities of the earth, that of Sarah and that of Hannah.

---

[70] Genesis 1:26
[71] Genesis 2:6

# YOM KIPPUR

## Authorized Cover-Up

**Mother Fire kindles us on Yom Kippur,** as fire consumes, transforms. On Yom Kippur we fast, we kindle the flames within us to burn-up not only our calories but also the stuff we wish to let go of and move on from into a new year of doing better, of doing things differently. Conversely, our wrongdoings, our mistakes, are in themselves a consuming fire, eating away at our potentials like a forest fire (*kee bo'arah ka'aish rish'ah*) – "for not-niceness burns like fire."[72] Yom Kippur is an opportunity to redirect our inner fires, our passions, our creativity, and temper them or fan them, whichever might be more of what we need. Fire either consumes or creates, destroys or reshapes, solidifies or implodes – our choice. On Yom Kippur we are on fire, purging and being purged, shaping and reshaping ourselves and welding it in place as the next yearly cycle unfolds. We bring our Fire of Heart into balance with the earlier Wind of Rosh Hashanah, and

---

[72] Isaiah 9:17

then, so that we don't smolder, we will next dampen the flames with the waters of Sukkot.

The Torah describes the primary offering for Yom Kippur as simply "A Fire Offering onto God."[73] Fire represents ignition, igniting, initiating, beginning something totally new from out of seemingly nothing – taking a daring step into the unknown Next moment, like God in that moment within non-time right before the onset of Genesis. It is a lonely moment. There is no one but yourself, hovering over the primal waters, hesitating over the power of possibility whose waves thrash beneath you waiting for you to draw possibility to realization. Fire is fueled from below (earth), and drawn from above (sky); it represents the kiss of heaven and earth, of spirit and matter, of your known self and your yet-unknown self that waits to unfold.

It is a misunderstanding of the Hebrew language that has many presuming that Yom Kippur purifies us. We don't need to be purified. Purification implies contamination, and we are not contaminated. The Hebrew word for what we customarily call "pure" is טָהֹר *te'har*, which at its root implies "Clear" as in "Cleared Space," or טְהִירוּ *te'heeru*, which is how the Kabbalah describes the great emptiness which God

---

73 Leviticus 23:27

first hollowed-out of the Nothing, and within which Creation then began.[74]

This is what Yom Kippur is about: a ceremony of Clearing, of hollowing-out a space within our deepest depths that is cleared of all impediments to our forward flow in the continuum of Creation, in the fruition of our Genesis. This is a much "clearer" translation of this ancient word than "Purified." *Purified* implies that we were contaminated. *Cleared* implies that we were overwhelmed, overfilled, over-circuited – for better or for worse -- which is the root meaning of the very word usually translated as "**Im**pure" or "Contaminated" – טָמֵא (*ta'may*). טָמֵא is rooted in the word טוּם (*toom*), which means "Filled." Another such badly translated word is גִּלּוּל (*gee'lul*), often rendered as either "Idolatry" or "Contamination," while it is rooted in the word גָּלַל (*ga'lal*), which means "Disregard" or "Oblivion."

Now let's read the famous passage from the Talmud, with these more accurate, albeit non-party-line root translations:

אָמַר רַבִּי עֲקִיבָא: «אַשְׁרֵיכֶם יִשְׂרָאֵל! לִפְנֵי מִי אַתֶּם מְטַהֲרִין וּ מִי מְטַהֵר אֶתְכֶם?
אֲבִיכֶם שֶׁבַּשָּׁמַיִם, שֶׁנֶּאֱמַר ‹וְזָרַקְתִּי עֲלֵיכֶם מַיִם טְהוֹרִים וּ טְהַרְתֶּם. מִכָּל טֻמְאוֹתֵיכֶם

---

[74] Zohar, Vol. 1, folio 15a and *Hashmato't HaZohar*, Vol. 1, folio 251a

וּמִכָּל גִּלּוּלֵיכֶם אֲטַהֵר אֶתְכֶם (יחזקאל לו:כה).› וְאוֹמֵר ›מִקְוֵה
יִשְׂרָאֵל יה (ירמיהו יז:יג)‹ מַה מִּקְוֶה
מְטַהֵר אֶת הַטְּמֵאִים, אַף הַקָּדוֹשׁ בָּרוּךְ הוּא מְטַהֵר אֶת יִשְׂרָאֵל

> Said Rabbi Akiva: "How fortunate are you, O Israel! Before whom do you become cleared, and who is it that clears you? Your Father Who is in Heaven! As it is written, 'And I shall cast upon you waters of clearing, and you will be cleared. I shall clear you of all of your overwhelmingness and of all of your oblivion'" (Ezekiel 36:25). And it is said, 'God is Israel's Ritual Pool [*mikveh*]' (Jeremiah 17:13). Just like the *mikveh* clears the overwhelmed, so does the Holy Blessed Source clear Israel.'"[75]

Yom Kippur is one day in the year when we are reminded of what we ought to be doing **every** day of the year: clearing out the gunk that builds up within us so that we can inhale fresh life-breath and refill our deepest core selves with the ever-renewing energies of Genesis. This is why we fast on this day. We are, again, clearing-out our body selves as we ritually clear-out our spirit selves. In the Torah, the act of fasting on Yom Kippur is described in most English translations as "You shall **afflict** your souls"[76] when the very same word for "you shall afflict" – תְּעַנּוּ (*ta'a'nu*) -- can just as easily translate as "you shall

---

[75] *Talmud Bav'li, Yoma* 85b
[76] Leviticus 16:29

**respond**," as in "You shall **respond** to your souls." Yom Kippur asks us not only to clear a new space within us and in our fields for a new yearly cycle of fresh plantings. It also asks us to plant new saplings over the old growth, to cover-up what *was* with what is yet waiting to *become*. Our past mistakes, our past overwhelmingness, our past obliviousness, will never go away. They can never be undone. But what we **can** do is cover them up with fresh soil for new growth, so that we transform what was **not** so good toward fertilizing that which can be **better**. As is written: "Happy is the One whose errors have been carried away, whose sins have been covered-up."[77]

This is the actual meaning of the word כְּפוּר (*kippur*). Ordinarily, we have been translating it as "Atonement." At its root, however, it means "To Cover," or "To Overlay," from the word כַּפְרָא (*kaf'ra*) or כַּפֹּרֶת (*ka'po'ret*) – which is how the Kabbalah speaks of the vegetative covering we are to use for the roof of our *Sukkah*. We are to use not freshly-purchased bamboo shoots or freshly-cut pine branches, but rather the *refuse* of our harvest, what of our harvest we do not wish to store for the future. Instead of throwing it away, we are to **use** the refuse, the rejects of our past deeds, of our past harvest, as the very sacred roof

---

[77] Psalms 32:1

covering for our very sacred *Sukkah* – to transform our past negativity into present and future positivity.

The disconnected branches and foliage with which we cover the roofs of our *Sukkot*, in other words, represent the spoils of our harvest[78] and thus also of our errors which we have let go of during Yom Kippur, disconnected from their roots – from deep within us – and now transformed into sacred implements intended to shelter us from our sense of being judged, intended to represent the compassionate sheltering of אמא עלאה *ema ila'a* – "Great Mother."[79]

Wait...slow down...Great *Who*? *What*? Wait. Are we still talking, like, *Jewish*?

Well, we are still talking, like, *Creation*, in sharing the Aboriginal *Jewish* Wisdom behind the so-called High Holydays, a month-long celebration of Beginningness. And the only God-Name mentioned in our people's *Creation* Story – Genesis, Chapter One – is אֱלֹהִים *Elo'heem*. And *Elo'heem*, our mystics taught us long ago "She is Great Mother...Mother of All, Mother of All Living."[80]

---

[78] *Menorat HaMa'or*, Vol. 3, Part 4, Ch. 1

[79] Zohar, Vol. 1, folio 22a and Vol. 2, folio 186b and Vol. 3, folio 100b, etc. etc. etc.

[80] *Tikunei Zohar*, folio 63b

אֱלֹהִים *Elo'heem* is that attribute of What-Cannot-Be-Named that called corporeal existence into becoming. It is the only Name associated with the unfolding of Creation. Literally, it is a plural word and implies "Who is of Itself and by Whose Will All is Possible."[81] As Creator aspect of God, *Elo'heem* is also referred to in much of our shamanic tradition as אֵימָא עִלָאָה *ey'ma ila'ah*, "Mother [of] Above," or "Great Mother." The God-Name revealed in the Creation story -- אֱלֹהִים -- is therefore in plural form because Creation involves spirit and matter, light and darkness, female and male, Heaven and Earth, as well as everything and its opposite, thus plural, as is written: "This too opposite the other did *Elo'heem* create."[82] Or: "I am *Hawayah*[83] and there is none else; Who forms the light and creates the darkness; maker of peace and creator of evil. I am *Hawayah* Who does **all** of these."[84] *Elo'heem*, then, is inclusive of all plurality. She is the force behind the tension of opposites. The

---

[81] בַּעַל הַיְכוֹלֶת וּבַעַל הַכֹּחוֹת כֻּלָם 16th-century Rabbi Yosef Karo in *Shulchan Aruch, Orach Chayyim* 5:1

[82] Ecclesiastes 7:14

[83] We have chosen הַוָיָה *Hawayah* to be used in referring to the text's mention of the ineffable God-Name יְהֹוָה *YHWH* in the place of the usual and quite irrelevant "Lord." In the words of the 18th-century Rebbe Nachmon of Breslav: "For the Holy Blessed One is called הַוָיָה *Hawayah*, for it was with the הַוָיָה *Hawayah* Name [referring to יְהֹוָה] that all of the universes became" (*Seehot HoRaN*, Chapter 95).

[84] Isaiah 45:6-7

tension of emergence kicks within her womb, waiting for her to call it forth, to **invite** it into becoming.[85] She is Great Mother, at the same time a Singular Self and Creator of Other. She is One, and She is Many. The perfect, singular balance of opposite polar forces is indeed wondrous, "what the mouth cannot speak and what the ear cannot hear."[86] *Elo'heem* is then an expression of the imminent mystery of the Ineffable, of what we call "God," but is not in Itself God; it is not an attempt to grasp, name or peg God. In the words of Abraham Joshua Heschel, "while God is a mystery, the mystery is not God."[87] In other words, to the claim that "God is everything," we say "But everything is not God."

Bottom line, the ancients of our people acknowledged the primal role of the forces of the feminine in the translation of the ineffable mystery of the beginning of the beginning, but they did not invent this concept out of thin air. *Elo'heem* by itself is neither a Him nor a Her, but in Its action mode, in its drama of creating, is in She mode as we see in the very opening narrative of Genesis where *Elo'heem* is described in feminine vernacular: "And the Spirit of *Elo'heem*, **She** *was hovering* over the Waters." The

---

[85] Zohar, Vol. 1, folio 16b

[86] *Talmud Bav'li, Shavu'ot* 20b

[87] *Man is Not Alone*, p. 237

word for "hovering" is here notably in the feminine -- מְרַחֶפֶת *M'ra'hefett*. And out of this was born the concept of אֵימָא עֵלָאָה Mother of Above, or Beyond, meaning that *Elo'heem,* as the act of God Creating, is Mother.

Now, let us return to Yom Kippur.

*Kippur* כִּפּוּר also means "To Erase," to clean the slate, so to speak, from the word כָּפַר *ka'far.* It is then a liberating festival, during which we are given another chance at having a go at it again. It is not a solemn day, but a celebrative one. After all, the ancient rabbis taught us that we ought to enter Yom Kippur with first having had a festive, **celebratory** feast just before Yom Kippur begins, and to do so in honor of **celebrating** Yom Kippur. In the words of the 16th-century Rabbi Moshe Cordovero:

> It is the way of all of Israel to rejoice on the eve of Yom Kippur, for every *mitzvah* requires the accompaniment of joy. Thus did the ancient sages declare that one who rejoices with festive eating and drinking on the eve of Yom Kippur is considered as if they had fasted all of both the ninth and tenth day of the month.[88] Because without rejoicing on the ninth (the eve of Yom Kippur), the festival is without joy since we are fasting on that day, whereas by eating and drinking festively on the eve of Yom Kippur, we

---

[88] *Talmud Bav'li, Yoma* 81b

infuse **all** of Yom Kippur with the requisite of joy necessary for sacred ritual.[89]

And let's not forget the teaching of the first-century Rabbi Shim'on ben Gamli'el: "No days were as festive in Israel as were the fifteenth of the Moon of *Ahv,* and Yom Kippur."[90] Why all this slop-happy reference to Yom Kippur? Because Yom Kippur is a reminder of God's intimate gesture to us, as is written: "He places his left hand beneath my head."[91] And almost immediately following Yom Kippur comes *Sukkot,* the phase of engaging, of intimate foreplay, as in: "And with his right arm he embraces me."[92] And *Sukkot* is followed immediately by *Sh'mee'nee Atzeret* שמיני עצרת, the Eighth Day of Closure, the conclusion of all the festivals of this month, representing the actual union, the climactic phase of lovemaking between Creator and Creation.[93]

---

[89] *Avodat Yom Hakippurim*

[90] *Mishnah, Ta'anit* 4:8

[91] Solomon's Song of Songs 2:6

[92] Song of Songs 2:6

[93] Zohar, Vol. 3, folio 257b

# Day of the Great Dragon

Sometimes, all hell breaks loose in the world-at-large or in our personal lives, leaving in its wake shattered hopes, broken faith, sabotaged dreams, smoldering disappointments and burning questions. Miraculously, though, the stench of tragedy eventually dissipates, and life goes on. The ancients explained it this way: "When the Great Dragon is hungry, his breath emits a flaming fire that is so hot and fierce that it brings the waters of the Abyss to a boil. And were it not that he is always resting his head in the Garden of Eden, no one could survive the stench of his breath."[94]

The Great Dragon is known in our mystery wisdom as תנינעוור *Taniniver,* literally: "Blind Dragon." And because he is blind, he has a serpent riding on his back, guiding him as he journeys across the Great Hollow of Possibility. His dwelling place, however, is in the realm of antithesis, the realm of oppositeness, of challenge. Oppositeness is not always a negative connotation, as it is not only an antithesis to its Other, it is also an important factor in the dynamics of **balancing** its Other.

---

[94] *Talmud Bav'li, Baba Bat'ra* 75a

*Taniniver*'s most **important** role is to mediate the dynamism between two mega-spirits who play vital roles in the rise or fall of the human enterprise. In fact, *Taniniver* is responsible for arranging the intimate union between these two mega-spirits, setting the time, the place, the venue, perhaps even the atmosphere for their lovemaking.[95]

Without *Taniniver*, not only would these two mega-spirits often neglect to bond, but they would also wreak havoc across the cosmos when they **did**. We know these two mega-spirits as Sama'el and Lilith, representative of the masculine and feminine forces of seductive illusion. Seductive illusion is the drama of subliminally getting you to see or believe something **is** when in reality it is **not**, or that something is **not** when in reality it **is**. Seductive illusion is being convinced beyond the shadow of doubt that you did the **right** thing only to discover down the road that what you did was **wrong**, or that you did the **wrong** thing only to discover down the road that what you did was **right**.

Sama'el and Lilith are so enthralled by and engrossed in their "trickster" work within the

---

[95] 16th-century Rabbi Moshe Cordovero in *Pardes Rimonim, Sha'ar* 25, Ch. 5 and 17th-century Rabbi Naftali ben Ya'akov Ha'Kohen in *Ey'mek Ha'melech*, folio 84b

melodramatic arena of human frailty that they rarely make time for each other. You might say that while they are believed to be a loving couple in a wholesome relationship, they are also workaholics. And by way of their mastery at seductive illusion, they feed on and are nurtured by our vulnerability and our gullibility, busily calling our bluff and putting our deepest convictions to the test.

In some religions, these two and what they represent are perceived in a negative light so that Sama'el is deemed "Satanic" and Lilith "Demonic." But in the Jewish mystery traditions, they are important holy divinely-ordained forces necessary for the evolution and ennoblement of the human spirit even as they endeavor to dampen and inhibit it.

Sama'el is all angel, and as such, he weaves Creator's intent into the life of Creation like any other angel and even serves as Keeper of the planet *Ma'a'deem* – or "Mars." He is the Trickster Angel who seduced First Woman into tasting of the Forbidden Fruit. He is described as being Master of Transparency, bereft of any degree of inhibition, totally free of every possible emotion of hindrance, whether guilt or remorse. He has no regrets, no neuroses, nothing is wrong with him. He is crystal clear. So crystal clear in fact that in 17 words he was able to undo God's **18** words and permit what God forbade. If you count the words in the original Hebrew text of the Torah, God instructs Adam and Eve not to eat of the Tree of Knowledge in 18 words, and Snake – the guise in which Sama'el appeared to them – got them to violate the instruction in 17 words. He is the Master of Illusion par-excellence. He can help us justify anything, do anything, see anything, believe anything, without even so much as a single fib.

Being a masculine force, Sama'el is drawn primarily to the feminine, which is why he approached **Eve** rather than Adam. He knows how to win a woman's heart far better than some mortal guy with issues. Adam's attempt at wooing Eve went nowhere. She says nigh a word to him throughout the entire story. Adam tries, but doesn't know how to relate. He doesn't know how to engage Eve in dialogue. **Sama'el** knows. Sama'el asks her a question, elicits response from her, kindles dialogue with her, and **challenges** her. All Adam says is "You are bone of **my** bone, babe, flesh of **my** flesh"[96] -- like it's all about **him**. Everything in regard to **her** is about **him** or in **relation** to him.

Sama'el, on the other hand, makes Eve feel that it's about **her**, as in "when you taste of that fruit, *hon*, your eyes are gonna open, your jaws will drop, you

---

[96] Genesis 2:23

will know things you've never known before. You will become liberated from the humdrum of oblivion."

Sama'el's success with the feminine is further illustrated by his successful relationship with Lilith. Lilith is the masculine's most intimidating antithesis. Adam was introduced to Lilith before Eve arrived on the scene, but their romance, as passionate as it flared, failed when Adam insisted on being on top, a position in lovemaking which **Lilith** demanded for herself. And so, failing to resolve the conflict, Lilith **abandoned** Adam, and God had to start all over by re-creating the human out of the clay again, this time as an equally male and female being in a singular shared body, a hermaphrodite, out of which God then separated the feminine part from the masculine part and embodied both as woman and man, respectively, or *Adam* and *Havah*. Thus, Genesis Chapter Two versus Genesis Chapter One. But that's a whole other story....

The arrival of Eve of course infuriated Lilith when she got wind of the news and she vowed to sabotage their relationship and any issue that would result from it – meaning, kids – and so she transmuted into an entity that became part mortal and part angel, what in our tradition we call a שֵׁד *shay'd*, and thus capable of dancing between **both** worlds.[97] In the

---

[97] *Alfa-Beita D'Ben Sira*, Ch. 5

radical Kabbalah of the 16th-century Rabbi Isaac Luria Ashkenazi, Lilith – all of her negative associations notwithstanding – is representative of a messianic hope of resolution and restoration of balance betwixt the sexes. She is the archetype of that aspect of the Feminine which terrifies the Masculine, and with which man is to endeavor to reconcile within his male psyche as part of the overall redemptive process.

The ancient rabbis openly admitted that in general, men are intimidated and thus uncomfortable with women who exhibit overt prowess, who are aggressive, preferring women who are passive and cooperative, yielding to man's desire and need for control and dominance. Adam's **first** woman companion, Lilith, exerted herself and refused to allow him his preferred sense of dominance. Adam's **second** woman companion in this myth is – in his mind -- "an improved edition," as powerful as Lilith but choosing instead to live in harmony with and in cooperation with Adam's masculine eccentricity. "Flesh of **my** flesh," he says about her, jumping up and down with joy. "Bone of **my** bone." And he names her accordingly: "Mother of all Living," because she finally made his world come alive – that is, of course, on **his** terms.

But Lilith – according to this school – hasn't retired to some demonic realm. Not at all. On the contrary, she cunningly incarnates and reincarnates throughout our history in the persona of the greatest of our women, sneaking into the life of Adam without him noticing. She first shows up in Leah, Jacob's first wife. Jacob, this tradition goes on to tell us, is a reincarnation of Adam and is therefore unhappy around Leah/Lilith. She is too aggressive for him, too **out**going: "And Leah **went out** to greet Jacob...."[98] In one instance, she barters with her sister Rachel for an extra night with their shared husband Jacob: "You must sleep with me. I have hired you with my son's mandrakes."[99] Rachel, on the other hand, is endearing to Jacob. He is smitten by her. While Leah's focus is on bedding Jacob (just like Lilith demanded to be on top in the Adam story), Rachel just wants kids: "Give me children, or I'll die."[100] So you have Leah chasing Jacob who is chasing Rachel who is chasing the dream of spawning kids.

In the end, Jacob and Leah seem to have worked things out, that is, Jacob/Adam seems to have grown comfortable with his aggressive companion Leah/Lilith and was no longer threatened by her, and they both live in unison to a ripe old age and are buried together as a couple in the "Cave of the Couples" in

---

[98] Genesis 30:16

[99] Genesis 30:16

[100] Genesis 30:1-2

Hebron.[101] All of this is a foretelling of the Messianic Age, goes the teaching, when Adam and Lilith will become reunited and shall dwell together in harmony; when all that has been separated shall become restored to its primal unity.

This is why Ruth, who is the progenitor of the Davidic Messiah of the future, is not blessed by the elders with the traditional blessing of "May you be like Sarah and Rebecca," but specifically with the blessing of "May you be like Rachel and Leah (Eve and Lilith)"[102] – the combined ingredients of the Feminine that will one day become unified in harmonization along with the Masculine. "In that day, God will be one and its Name one."[103]

The Lurianic School goes much deeper and even has Jacob/Adam incarnating in the second-century Rabbi Akiva, whose wife, Rachel, personified the *biblical* Rachel and thus, by association, Eve as well. Later in his life, Akiva ends up marrying a more aggressive and overtly seductive woman who personified Lilith, namely a Roman convert named Rufina, formerly wife of the then-Roman governor of Judea, Quintus Tineius Rufus.[104]

---

[101] Genesis 49:29-31 and 50:13
[102] Ruth 4:11
[103] Zechariah 14:9
[104] *Talmud Bav'li, Ketuvot* 62b-63a

These and a host of other tidbits from this school portray Lilith in an arena of the struggle between the sexes and the hope that one day we will see an end to the battle for dominance and the beginning of the peace of mutual acceptance in regard to Self and Other and to the interplay of both.

As Sama'el is drawn primarily to women, Lilith is drawn primarily to men, making love to them in their dreams. Nor are these nocturnal rendezvous free from pregnancies. Rather, hordes of little Sama'els and Liliths emerge from them, further embellishing and empowering the forces of seductive illusion in the world. I mean, you can't expect those two to do it all alone. Lots of people in the world. So, as **our** population grows, so do **theirs**.

And now you know why everything is progressing beyond our wildest imagination while at the same time falling **apart** beyond our wildest imagination. Most of this seductive work is performed by Lilith, which explains why she's rarely home and *Taniniver* the Blind Dragon needs to make sure she and Sama'el have **some** private time together. As the sixteenth-century Kabbalist Rabbi Eliyahu de Vidas explained: "All the passions of the world come from Lilith, because Samael, who is on a very subtle level of existence [that is, all-spirit], does not have a way of taking hold of man, who is mostly matter. He therefore depends on Lilith, who [having once been mortal] retains physical attributes as well."[105]

So, to cap-off Lilith, she represents the mystery force of Nemesis within Genesis. She is לִילִית *"ley'lit,"* which is Night, and night is that part of Day which obscures, which blurs discernment, and blends (meaning of the Hebrew עֶרֶב *"erev"* for evening) and mixes truths with lies, light with dark, good with evil. And so, in the end of times, our prophet Yir'miyahu foresaw, "a new thing will God have made, in that Woman shall encircle Man,"[106] dramatized at most Jewish weddings in the ritual of the bride encircling the groom. In the end, Lilith will be the force which puts Humpty-Dumpty back together again and liberates us from misogyny.

What has all this to do with the High Holydays?

More than you can imagine.

The Turning of the Year, as it is called *Te'ku'fat Ha'Shanah,"*[107] is the turning of the head of the Great Dragon as he prepares the venue for the two troublemakers to leave us alone for a while so that **they**

---

[105] *Rey'sheet Chochmah, Sha'ar Ha'Yir'ah,* Ch. 8
[106] Jeremiah 31:22
[107] Exodus 34:22

can have some bonding time and so that **we** can clean up some of the messes they helped us make throughout the past year. And on Yom Kippur, we send them a snack to keep them busy -- the proverbial *Scapegoat*....

# The Scapegoat and the Illusionist

Have you ever had one of those days or nights during which you find yourself worrying for hours on end about a matter you're not even sure is actually cause for worrying? Say, the gas pump doesn't fill your tank all the way one day, and you interpret this to mean your credit card's been maxed which is impossible because you know you've got cash in the bank to cover it, so it could only mean that your account may have been hacked and you're now in the hole and have to call the bank in the morning to deal with all of this and get a whole new card and examine your bank statement to contest fraudulent charges, and you go to bed worrying, turning and twisting all night wondering how did this happen, and why, and what are you going to use to fill up your near-empty tank and get to work tomorrow and how are you going to buy groceries and pay the rent which is due in two days, not to mention the phone bill which is dangerously overdue and threatening to cut you off from all communication with the rest of Planet Earth?

And then, and then the next day you find out that actually your money's still in your account, **with** interest, and that it was probably just a faulty gas pump, and all is well, and you lost sleep – not to mention years off your designated life span -- worrying over absolutely nothing.

This may very well have been what happened to the Biblical character *Eee'yo'v* (a/k/a "Jo'b"). The Book of Jo'b is about some guy who had everything and then lost it all because of a wager God made with one of his top angels. Most of you know this angel as a **bad** sort of guy, namely "Satan," or "The Devil", or "Lucifer." Truth be told, he's had a bad rap, thanks to the zeal of religious hype and sorely misguided theologies. In our people's language he is known as הַשָּׂטָן *ha'satan*, literally: "The Obstructer." He is an angel like any other, with a mission assigned him by God Itself. His mission is to call your bluff and test your conviction. So be nice and stop blaming all your ills on him.

We are going to say this only once: *He **didn't** make you do it.*

*Ha'satan*'s wager with God was that he could get Jo'b so pissed-off that Jo'b would break down and reveal his true character from beneath all his purported "saintliness" and **curse** God. God then accepts the bet and authorizes *ha'satan* to go do his thing, which he does by stripping Jo'b of all of his assets, at home and abroad – including his hidden Hedge Funds – then striking him with some god-awful disease which caused him to lose his health insurance, and depriving him of everything and everyone he'd ever cherished. In the end, *ha'satan* **loses** the bet, but only after we've plowed through 37 chapters in which Jo'b and his friends philosophize around the question of why he had to endure all of this needless suffering in the **first** place, or why bad things happen to good people.

Now, what if Jo'b never actually lost **any**thing? What if none of what the story describes actually occurred, and Jo'b got sick from worrying as intensely as he did over what he ***believed*** had happened, but which in reality **didn't**? After all, nowhere in the entire story is there a clear indication that any of the stuff Jo'b was **told** happened, actually **happened**. All we are told is that some anonymous character or another showed up day after day with increasingly horrifying news alleging that such-and-such occurred. But never is there any mention of the occurrence ***itself*** outside of the hearsay delivered by a successive host of unnamed messengers.

Could it be that the unnamed characters who kept showing up in various guises with ever-intensifying news were none other than *ha'satan* and his cadre busily trying to **trip** Jo'b? Does Jo'b set off to investigate these reports? Does he attend so much as a single funeral? Not at all. He falls apart the moment he hears the reports, accepts them as truths, and descends deeper and deeper into a sink-hole of utter despair hollowed-out by the "reports." His suffering, his grieving, is so real that his friends come over to sit with him and comfort him, for they too have been swept up in the whirlwind that now has their hapless friend spinning out of control. And so, for 37 densely-worded chapters we are forced to listen to Jo'b and his well-meaning friends pontificate and theorize why it is that Jo'b has been strapped with a series of ghastly tragedies that may not even have occurred **after** all!

In the end, The *Satan* throwing up his arms in utter frustration, bored out of his angelic skull by all the philosophizing going on in Job's living room day after day but still feeling somewhat successful in that he at least got Jo'b to *think* he'd lost everything even though he hadn't lost **any**thing.

In the end, as the story has it, God appears to Jo'b "from out of the whirlwind," from out of the spin in which Jo'b had gotten himself tangled; from out of the storm of assumption and of all the havoc it had wrought. In the end, God does not **heal** Jo'b, because Jo'b isn't really sick. It's all in his head. Rather, Jo'b becomes "healed" by the spontaneous act of God wrenching him out of his spin, out of the illusion he had created for himself by way of his worry-ridden assumptions. Nor does God in the end answer Job's questions of "Why?" Because to respond to questions would be tantamount to acknowledging that there are any. And in truth, all of our questions about life are predicated upon assumptions we ourselves have invented or that have been invented for us by others just as clueless.

In the end, everything and everyone Jo'b thought he'd lost are restored to him manifold more than they were before, meaning he came away with a deeper appreciation for his daughters, his sons, his herds, his fields, his employees, and so on. Not that God waved a wand and suddenly daughters and sons appeared from out of nowhere to replace the ones that were allegedly gone. On the contrary, they appeared from where they'd been meandering all along. While Jo'b had been mourning them, they had been happily prancing about in Reno or the Caribbean, and his allegedly-abducted field workers had been joyfully gyrating at a Grateful Dead Concert in the Land of Oz. And no animals were hurt in the making of this story.

And if you are wondering in your skeptical mind how it is possible for such a holy and enlightened and spiritually evolved master like Jo'b to have fallen for *ha'satan*'s illusionistic tricks, and to such a **degree**! -- then remember how the Torah describes *ha'satan* in the guise of the Edenic Serpent as "the most cunning of all creations,"[108] so incredibly cunning, in fact, that he was able to successfully talk the first human couple into partaking of the very fruit of which they were specifically instructed by Creator just twenty minutes earlier *not* to partake. If Adam and Eve, the direct handiwork of God, could fall for the web of illusion spun by *ha'satan*, so much more so is it feasible that Jo'b could and would as well.

*Ha'satan* – or The Satan -- is an illusionist par-excellence. The best there is and ever was. It's his job; his role in the scheme of things; the very purpose for which he was created: to challenge always our snug take on reality, our convictions, our self-proclaimed truths and home-brewn presumptions. If he can dupe Adam and Eve, he can dupe Jo'b, and he can certainly pull the wool over **our** eyes.

Mystics like the 18th-century Rebbe Nachmon of Breslav, referred to The Satan as הַמְדַמֶּה כֹּחַ *ko'ah ha'me'dameh*, "The Force of Similitude," the force that can render what **is** as *not* and what is **not** as *is*. The Satan is the illusionist-*par-excellence*, capable of making nothing *appear* as if it were something, and something *appear* as if it were nothing. And it bears repeating that in the original Hebraic narrative of the

---

[108] Genesis 3:1

Adam and Eve story, it took Snake only *seventeen* words to undo what God had decreed in *eighteen* words. Because illusion, you see, is but only a single tiny step *short* of reality. It is close enough a degree of *Almost* to practically resemble with uncanny precision that which in reality it is not.

Nothing actually happened to Jo'b. The narrative does not describe anything actually **happening** to anyone, only that a series of messengers show up on Job's front porch with reports of one fiasco after the other.[109] The first of these "messengers" is described in the Hebrew as מַלְאָךְ *mal'ach* which translates both as "Messenger" and as "Angel" – take your pick. In other words, an angel – The Satan? – came to him with a report, and then another angel – of The Satan's crew? -- or The Satan in a variety of disguises? -- and then another and another. No mention of Jo'b dialing 9-1-1 and then dashing off to investigate, or to bury his supposedly dead children, or to gather neighbors and kinsmen to try and retrieve the stolen herds or abducted shepherds. He just falls apart on the spot and blesses God instead of cursing.

Failing to trip Jo'b and get him to *curse* God, Snake gets more physical and makes him think he's sick, and it's so real for him that he breaks out in boils,

---

[109] Job 1:14-18

but he still goes to *shul* and board meetings. This guy is hard to crack. You can **fool** him but you can't break him.

In the end, as in the beginning, Jo'b has three daughters and seven sons.[110] Nothing's changed. Nothing's changed because nothing happened. Nor does it say that God increased for Jo'b double of what he *lost*. Rather, it says "And God increased everything that was [already] unto Jo'b, double their number."[111] But he still had the same number of daughters and sons, except now Job's eyes are open, his heart has been renewed, he sees life differently, he has been redeemed from out of the whirlwind, a whirlwind which The Satan had fanned into a Tsunami but which Jo'b himself had seeded in presuming too much about what God wanted. So much so, in fact, that he would regularly offer up sin-offerings on behalf of his party-loving children just in case they got too naughty during one of their wild bashes.[112]

Not anymore, though. Following his debacle, Job has now been exposed to the God who is anything *but* exacting; to the God who leaves us ample room for error, and who would rather that Jo'b focus more on

---

[110] Job 1:2 and 42:13
[111] Job 42:11
[112] Job 1:5

the needs of his family not in terms of what he assumes they owe God, but in terms of what it is they owe themselves for bettering the quality of their lives. Jo'b becomes more sensitive to the honor and dignity of his daughters, for instance, than constantly worrying about the honor of God. God cannot be slighted, Jo'b learns; but **people** can. Having now learned this after his lengthy and intensive stroll with God who cherishes her Creations in Chapters 38 and on, Job's daughters are now *named*, and described as "the most beautiful in all the land," and apportioned their own 20-acre homesteads whereas in the beginning they were nameless squatters at the homes of their equally nameless and anonymous brothers.[113]

The wool over our eyes, you see, can either leave us forever blinded and weighed down or gift us with renewed vision and fortitude. It is up to us, to how we respond once we realize we've been duped. We can in that moment fall, or rise. "And the eyes of them both [Adam and Eve] were awakened, and they became aware that they were naked."[114] Adam and Eve did indeed push through the wool that was pulled over their eyes by Snake – a/k/a *Sama'el*; a/k/a *HaSatan* -- and they did indeed come out the other side, like Jo'b

---

[113] Job 1:4
[114] Genesis 3:7

would, and with fresh, renewed perspective.[115] ("Original Sin" is in neither the vocabulary nor the theology of the tradition in which that story originated.)

The Illusionist, you see, thrives on our attachment to the world of imagery and appearances, on our draw to or repulsion from what things "look like" or "sound like" or "feel like." He takes advantage of our obsession with expression, with mastering the art of communication, our self-confidence or the lack thereof. He is after all the first of God's creations to initiate, to take a first step, to open communications. He invented **Question**. He kindled **Response**. He developed **Dialogue**. He was the most "naked" of all creatures, reads the original Hebrew narrative in its literal translation.[116] Cunning *schmunning*. He was more ***naked*** than anything God ever created, meaning he was so totally emotionally and intellectually honest and open that you'd have wanted to marry him straightaway ***regardless*** of your sexual orientation. He is The Illusionist, the *ko'ach ha'me'dah'meh*, the Power of Similitude.

And you can't live with him or without him. Not in ***this*** world. Not in the Garden of Paradox. He is your ticket to Heaven or to Hell -- which are in essence one

---

[115] *Midrash Pesikta D'Rav Kahane* 23:1

[116] Genesis 3:1

and the same -- for he is willing to negotiate your trip to either for the same price. He is your guide to the Tree of Life or the Tree of Knowledge – which are in essence one and the same tree -- for he is naked, more naked than you can possibly imagine, and he enjoys helping you see what you want to see. And to keep himself as naked as possible he sheds his skin periodically, and like a master initiating a disciple, he drops his shed skin for you to find and to don, for you to wear over your own nakedness lest you become overwhelmed by it. This way, you can walk about making-believe you're as naked as he, while all along veiling all that you prefer not to expose of your deepest Shadow Self.

He is the spiritual embodiment of all that is homeopathic. He is poison; he is medicine. He calls your bluff. He puts your conviction to the test. He is The *Satan*, an extremely high and important Angel of God who has been demonized by religion and tabooed by most of humankind through most of human history. He is סָמָאֵל Sama'el, סָמָא *sama* meaning "blinding," and also "potion." Potions can heal; potions can kill. Darkness is blinding, and so is too much Light. He is the juggler of both ends of the same stick, Keeper of Polarities, Dancer of the Spectrums, Master of Illusions. He is neither good nor evil. He is both.

And in very ancient times, on *Yom Kippur* –the holiest of the holiest of days for the Jewish people -- we used to invite him to our Ceremony of Atonement and accord him an equal share of the main dish we served Creator: Goat. We sent one goat to God, and one to The Illusionist, both goats symbolic of all of The Illusionist's successes in causing us to stumble and trip all over ourselves, causing us to feel that what we did wrong was okay – in the moment – and then leaving us hanging with the pain of regret and the anguish of remorse the morning after. And for this, we rewarded him with what has over time come to be known as a "scapegoat," a sort of bribe to "destroy the original negatives."

The ritual of selecting which goat was to be offered to God and which to The Illusionist played-out like a public magic show, a performance in which the High Priest appeared to take the place of The Illusionist. He stood in front of a small box in which lots were placed, two pieces of boxwood inscribed either with the words "For יהוה *YHWH*" or the words "For עֲזָאזֵל *Aza'zel*."[117] Two goats were then positioned on either side of him, one to his left and one to his right. He would then reach into the box and mix up the pieces so that he no longer knew which one was for the goat on the right, which for the goat on the left. Then he

---

[117] Leviticus 16:8-10 and 21-23

blindly reached both hands into the box and quickly, spontaneously, and without thinking about it or in any way hesitating, withdrew both pieces of boxwood simultaneously, one in each hand. If, for instance, his left hand held the piece marked "For *YHWH*," the goat on his left would be designated for the altar and the goat on the right for *Aza'zel*, and vice-versa.[118]

After sending the spirit of the one goat to God, the High Priest would then lay his hands upon the **second** goat, the "scapegoat" – actually referred to in the Hebrew as שָׂעִיר הַחַי *se'ir ha'chai* -- "**Living** Goat" – and assign it into the care of a designated אִישׁ עִתִּי *eesh ee'tee*, literally: "A Man of Season,"[119] meaning someone who is ready, prepared, really present in the moment to engage whatever, whenever, however. The ancient mystics described this character as having bushy eyebrows, blue eyes that were crooked and asymmetrical, with one eye being smaller than the other.[120] These facial features would indicate to the High Priest that he was the right man for the job (and don't ask us why). The bushy eye-browed, blue-eyed, crooked-eyed, asymmetrical-eyed designee would then lead the Living Goat across the Judean hills way into the nakedness place, to an undesignated designated

---

[118] *Talmud Bav'li, Yoma* 37a and *Mishnah, Yoma* 3:10

[119] Leviticus 16:21

[120] Zohar, Vol. 3, folio 63b

site in the desert, where he would release the goat to the **Master** of Nakedness, The Illusionist, referred to by the Torah narrative as "Aza'zel." And *wa la*! ***Poof***! Sins are gone. Vanished!

In this annual drama of the Day of Atonement, God represents the actual dissipation of our sins while Aza'zel represents the earthly fact that even though our sins are no more, there remain ample memories of them strewn all about the labyrinth of our ongoing life journey – in the backroads of the memories of our minds, as the song goes -- for, again, we live in the realm of attachments, and it's hard to let go, to truly **truly** let go. The "Living Goat" who symbolically carries our mistakes into the desert, into the void, takes them as far away as possible, out of sight, but is still a "living" goat nonetheless. Our past is gone, vanished, but what carries it is still alive, trekking through the wilderness toward Aza'zel in the hope that The Illusionist will, again, "burn the negatives" and free us of what he otherwise lords over our heads—or of what we call "guilt."

Whether all of this is to be taken literally or not is moot against the awesome backdrop of the wisdom gleaned from this primitive shamanic ceremony. The ancient teachers read into it any number of concepts and interpretations because that's our way. We don't just make bread out of the raw gift of wheat or barley. We also make cupcakes and cereal and beer. Likewise, the sages drew from a rainbow of perspectives, some seeing the Aza'zel ceremony as a gesture of atonement for the Fallen Angels of Genesis 6:4 who symbolize the overwhelming force of the sensuous. The sensuous, they felt, often burns so fiercely within us that we are led to make wrong choices out of the sway of our natural terrestrial impulses, impulses so potent they even lured Heavenly Angels out of their hoity-toity celestial Paradise.[121] Others saw the ritual as the necessary act of inviting the forces of evil into the ceremony of the sacred as a gesture of unifying all of the polarities of our mysterious universe.[122] And yet others, like the 18th-century Rabbi Shimshon Rafael Hirsch, interpreted the rite as very directly addressing the day-to-day downhome nitty-gritty in-the-moment struggle of right or wrong choice-making:

> Clearly, we have here a description of two creatures which at the outset are identical in every respect but which come to a complete parting of the ways once they arrive at the threshold of the Sanctuary. They are both identical in appearance, size and monetary value. Both were purchased at the same time. Both are placed in the same manner "before

---

[121] *Talmud Bav'li, Yoma* 67b; Book of Enoch 10:4,5
[122] Zohar, Vol. 3, folio 63a

God in the entrance of the Tent of Appointed Meeting." The lot marked "for God" or that "for Aza'zel" could fall upon either one of them. The chances of becoming the one or the other are the same for each. Indeed, each of the two can only become that which it will become because it could just as well have become the other.…..
Thus, all of us are placed into the entrance of His Sanctuary, without distinction [to decide] between YHWH and Aza'zel, between God and the powers of our senses.…This choice is not made for any of us in advance. Physical appearances, physical stature, financial status, higher or lower social standing, greater or lesser affluence, even the circumstances under which we are called upon to make our choices – none of these have a compelling influence on our decision. Respected or obscure, great or humble, rich or poor, today or tomorrow, no matter what his powers or possessions – anyone can become either "onto YHWH" or "onto Aza'zel" at any time…. Indeed, the very enticements of Aza'zel should have led him to God, for without these temptations he could never have become the free-willed [son or daughter] and servant of God, of the free-willed Holy One.[123]

However you slice it, it boils down to this: We are all cast into a narrow box in which we meander about between two pieces of boxwood, one marked for

---

[123] *The Pentateuch* [Abridged One-Volume Version], pp. 436-438

God, one for Aza'zel. This is what it looks like inside of us. On the outside, we stand tall and majestic, like the High Priest of antiquity, ready to chance our next move with an air of awe and audacity. Two equally attractive or equally foreboding choices are brought to us and positioned on either side of us as we take a deep breath and quickly reach into our deepest innards with both possibilities in mind and do our best with whatever and however the consequences of our action might turn out. In most every choice we make, we have to end up sending a part of our Self out to the unknown perils of the wilderness abode of Aza'zel, even if we first sent another part of our Self to the highest and most noble reaches of intents – that is, even if we made the most correct and most gallant of choices.

In every choice, then, there is sacrifice, for better or for worse, or for both. This underlies all of the rituals of the sacrificial rites of our early ancestors. They were meant to teach us this important life lesson. The altars, the animals, the blood, the dead-bird/live-bird rituals, the live-goat/dead-goat rituals, the red-cow-ashes rituals, the sacred fire and incense rituals -- all of them were intended not for the altars of earth and stone but for the far more sacred altars of heart and soul. Their mysteries remain precious and have empowered us to survive thousands of years of disillusionment, because they remain always the antidote to the cunningness of The Illusionist; they remain always the trick in tricking the Trickster.

Jo'b, you see, was a passionate, devoted ritual-sacrificer. He had one sacrifice or another smoldering on his altar almost every other day, bribing God to forgive his party-loving kids just in case they erred. Just in case. He had no idea whether they actually did or not. He was tangled-up in the power of illusion and assumption. All of his subsequent questions regarding what God did or didn't do to him, or should or shouldn't have done, were all predicated on his illusory presumptions about God, Life, and Job. He was so totally a victim of The Illusionist that all it took The Satan to get him grieving and sick was hearsay, some anonymous Blog, something he'd read on Google or seen on YouTube.

Yom Kippur is more than an ancient biblical Israelite ceremony. It is a universal lesson that reminds us to transform our Scapegoat Selves into *Living* Goats, and The Illusionist into our Teacher. *With* him alone we **are** nothing, for he overshadows our Selfhood. With*out* him altogether we *learn* nothing, for he also *empowers* our Selfhood. It all depends on whether we stand up there like an *Almost*-High-Priest with only *one* piece of boxwood in the container before us and one solitary goat by our side, or whether we stand boldly as the fully-empowered and anointed High Priest before the concealed encasement of Choice with two unequalled pieces of boxwood and two **equal** goats at either side, ready to walk the tightrope between the Angel of Light and the Angel of Darkness, remembering always that both work for the same boss and that both have your best interest in mind and that both are actually one and the same and that their seeming difference is nothing more than an...illusion... no less than the man with the big eye and the small eye is still one and the same guy, his asymmetrical eyes, bushy eyebrows and crooked glance notwithstanding.

To get this difficult concept across with a tad more clarity, there is the ensuing story of Plimo.[124]

---

[124] *Talmud Bav'li, Kidushin* 81a

# Plimo

Plimo was a righteous man who lived in Jerusalem in the first century, B.C.E. He was a wealthy and very successful merchant known for his charitable ways, and he was blessed with a beautiful family and a huge, luxurious abode. As part of his daily religious devotion, he would ask God to please keep The Satan away from him and from his family, and then he would proclaim: "An arrow in your eye, O Dark Angel!" And thus he went about satisfied that he'd driven away any impulse toward sinfulness by his daily bold appellations against The Illusionist.

One Yom Kippur Eve, when Plimo sat comfortably around his dinner table surrounded by his honorable guests and his perfect family, a filthy disheveled vagabond arrived, knocking ferociously on Plimo's 2,100-year-old door. As you know, on the eve of this holiest day of the year we are encouraged to celebrate with a lavish feast as is befitting a festival such as this, to remind us that even though we will be fasting during the entire day from nightfall to nightfall, it is still a *festive* period, as we rejoice in our faith that our past sins will be erased on that very day and that our credit will be good once again.

And so there they sat, eating and drinking, Plimo at the head of the table all bedecked in his finest and feeling beside himself, in a *good* way, when this repulsive scrounger comes knocking in the middle of this most sacred feast. Plimo, being the pious and benevolent patron that he was, rose immediately from the comfort of his cushions, swung open the door, and brought the stranger a plate of delicacies and some bread, even some wine, and placed it on his front porch for the man to sit and eat there.

No sooner had Plimo sat back down at the table inside the house when he heard the strange stranger begin to snarl and grumble.

"So!!" the man yelled, "everyone sits on cushions inside the comfort of the house and I have to sit out here on this wooden bench?!"

Plimo rose up, went outside, apologized to the man and invited him inside and, because of his stench, seated him in a corner some distance, from the dinner table. No sooner had Plimo rejoined his guests when he heard the beggar begin to snarl and grumble again.

"So!!" the man yelled, this time even louder, and foaming at the mouth, "everyone gets to sit together around the dinner table and I have to sit here in the corner all by my**self** like some kind of *reject*?!"

Plimo rose up again, apologized, and escorted the stranger to the table, much to the annoyance of his guests who by now were trying not to inhale too deeply due to the stench of urine, smoke and mildew. The man sat down on one of Plimo's favorite cushions, sipped from his goblet, then spat-out the wine in disgust. Then he dipped his filth-caked hand into the shared soup bowl to retrieve a chunk of meat, tasted it, and spat that out too.

Plimo had about had it up to and beyond "here." He rose up out of his cushions, walked over to the man, seized him by the arm, and began shouting angrily into his mud-covered ears: "How dare you come into my home and insult me, my family, my guests, my mother-in-law's cooking!! I have been more than gener...."

The man, shocked by the assault, choked on a piece of meat still in his mouth, dropped his plate, and fell to the floor, unresponsive.

Plimo knelt by the man, checked his pulse, ordered a feather be held over his nostrils, and, it then dawned upon him like a meteor crashing down from the skies that the stranger was *dead*, that he'd caused a man to *die*!!!!!! -- and on the eve of *Yom Kippur* to *boot*!!! Plimo up and dashed to his bedchamber where he dropped to the floor and wept profusely. He could ot believe it!! Here he was preparing to enter the holiest day of the year, the Day of **Atonement**! And he had lost his temper and *killed* a man!!! His entire life was ruined!! What was there to live for now!? How could he ever again celebrate Yom Ki….

His laments were suddenly interrupted by a gentle tap on his shoulder.

With great trepidation, Plimo turned around.

It was him. The beggar. The dead man. Except he wasn't dead, after all. Before Plimo could utter a sound, ask a question, express an emotion, the filthy, smelly, disheveled stranger began to shape-shift before his eyes, and within moments morphed into a beautiful, glowingly angelic being.

"But who…who…what…who are you?" Plimo could barely speak.

"I am *he*, the one you pray against daily, Plimo, the one in whose eyes you keep shooting imaginary arrows; the one you keep asking God to keep away from you and your family."

"You are **him**? The Satan? The Angel of Darkness? The Illusionist?"

"I am he."

"Why did you frighten me like this? You have no idea how terrified and hopeless and…I mean that was a horrific trick to pl…."

"Horrific, you say? Well, isn't that how you have thought of me all along? Isn't that the theme of your prayers about me? So what did you *expect*?"

"Well, what *should* I be praying about you?"

"Pray that God bless me in that the goodness he desires for his world be brought to its most optimal fruition by my working its opposite."

"But I thought that you…."

"That I am all about evil. Well, I will have you know that what I did to you tonight was a good thing, a precious gift, for until this moment you would have entered this holy of all days presuming you were righteous and sinless at the core, when all along, festering deep inside of you, was the potential to blow up at some poor helpless hungry beggar and have him thrown feet first out of your home. Now, however, that dormant sin has been externalized, cut out of you like a boil removed from a diseased person, and you can enter Yom Kippur clean and whole, a truly remorseful penitent who has confessed what he might never have had the opportunity to confess about himself, having for so long veiled it comfortably beneath self-righteousness and in the guise of religious piety. It is my job to call your bluff, and so I did. And now your Yom Kippur will be the most beautiful and most sacred and most meaningful than ever it was."

And with that, The Illusionist flapped his wings and flew off into the realms of the Great Unknown. And Plimo lived happily ever after, and never again uttered so much as a single negative word in regard to The Illusionist, for he had never been so enlightened by anyone as he had by the Angel of Darkness.

And as for the trauma Plimo experienced from what he *thought* had happened but that actually *didn't* in the way he *thought* it did – well, it shape-shifted into a Living Goat and wandered into the desert in search of Aza'zel. For only Aza'zel can take back a memory and destroy the negatives.

# Day of Intimacy

Yom Kippur a day of *intimacy*? Then why did the ancient wisdom keepers tells us not to make **love** on Yom Kippur?[125]

The deeper we delve into the meaning of Yom Kippur, the more it becomes about love and intimacy, not guilt and repentance. It is a sacred day of connecting to the root of roots, to the essence of our soul self, as is asked of us in the Torah's instruction regarding Yom Kippur: "And you should respond to your souls"[126] -- often translated as "And you shall **afflict** your souls." Which of the two renditions we choose is up to us, they are both grammatically and etymologically correct, which leaves us simply with the question: What kind of Yom Kippur do we want? Or better yet, what kind of relationship do we want with God, with Self, with Other? Affliction, or Response? Guilt, or Intimacy? Fear, or Love?

Not surprisingly, then, did the first-century Rabbi Shimon ben Gamliel referred to Yom Kippur as one of the most festive days on the Hebraic calendar.

---

[125] *Mishnah, Yoma* 8:1
[126] Leviticus 16:31

What happened on Yom Kippur back then to render it the happiest and most festive of Jewish holiday celebrations? "For on that day, the daughters of Jerusalem would go forth dressed in white borrowed garments, so as not to embarrass those who lacked, and each garment was first immersed in living waters to cleanse them of any stains; and the daughters of Jerusalem would then go forth and dance in the vineyards. And what did they chant? 'Young man! Lift up your eyes and observe -- what is it that you are discerning for yourself? Cast not your eyes upon our outer beauty; rather examine our family background....'"[127]

Later sages added the following: "Those women who prided themselves in their attractiveness declared 'Set your eyes upon our beauty!' Those who were of nobility declared 'Set your eyes on our family origins!' Those who considered themselves neither attractive nor of noble lineage declared: 'Take us for the sake of heaven but also adorn us with beautiful garments and ornaments while you're at it.'"[128]

We party and masquerade on Purim; spin the *dreidel* and oil our gullets on Hanukah; gorge ourselves with the finest cuisines on Passover; and yet we are told that none of these were considered among the

---

[127] *Mishnah, Ta'anit* 4:8
[128] *Talmud Bav'li, Ta'anit* 31a

most festive periods in ancient Israel? Rather, the mc festive days were Yom Kippur, which we presume was the most *solemn* day of the year and during which we abstained from food and drink, and some obscure date like the 15th of the Moon of *Ahv*. In addition, we're told that the particular ceremony that made those two days the most festive involved a gathering of single ladies dancing in the vineyards and chanting admonishments at single male gawkers?

It would then seem that what makes us happier than feasting on Passover or Purim is fasting on Yom Kippur. What gladdens our hearts more than dancing on *Simchat Torah* is dancing on a day of fasting and expiation of sins. And what better way to celebrate Yom Kippur than to send our single daughters out to dance in the vineyards while confounding single male onlookers (only those men who were not yet married were permitted to participate).[129]

One of the reasons for celebrating with such festivities on Yom Kippur, aside from the standard one about rejoicing in the faith that God has forgiven us on that day, is that Yom Kippur also commemorates the time Moses descended from the mountain after his third ascension, bringing down a second pair of tablets along with God's assurance of forgiveness over the

---

[129] *Talmud Bav'li, Ta'anit* 31a

olden Calf incident. The common thread in unraveling the mystery of this strange ritual -- strange, that is, for Yom Kippur – has to do with vineyards. Vineyards grow grapes. Grapes make wine. Wine makes people happy.[130] Wine was also the very first act of transformation, of alchemy, which Noah performed following the Great Deluge and in celebration of the restoration of an otherwise devastated planet.[131] So it is fitting that on Yom Kippur, when we rejoice in the faith that God has forgiven us for our errors of the past year, that the single women amongst us exchange clothing one with the other, and go out to dance and sing amid that attribute of our Earth that brings us gladness and that long ago enwombed the seed of restoration: the vineyard. It is also fitting that single men held the space for the women so that the joys of committed relationships, of companionship, can start to happen for them as well.

All of the women, we are told, wore simple white garments. "The daughters of royalty borrowed the garments of the daughters of the high priest. The daughters of the high priest borrowed garments from the daughters of the deputy high priest. The daughters of the deputy high priest borrowed garments from the daughters of the anointed warrior-priest. The daughters

---

[130] Psalms 104:15
[131] Genesis 9:20

of the anointed warrior-priest borrowed garments f.
the daughters of the common priests. And the daughte
of the non-priest Israelites borrowed garments fron.
one another so that no one would lack," and thus no
one could tell who was of what station.[132]

In this scenario, single men seeking wives were
confounded, confused, unable to determine who was
who. Most everyone looked alike on the outside. The
beautiful ones taunted them to pay attention to them
because of their beauty, which made the men wonder
about their personalities. The noble ones taunted them
to pay attention to their family of origin, which made
them wonder which was more advantageous in the
long run, attractiveness or family background. And
the not-so-attractive ones challenged the men to
examine their intentions – that if their hearts were
truly in a place of Godliness where looks didn't matter,
why not pick **them**? But at the same time, they shouldn't
think they would then get away with not having to buy
them fancy ornaments to beautify their outward
appearances.

And all of this was going on in the vineyards,
the places where wine was born. "When wine comes
in," goes an ancient rabbinic adage, "secrets come

---

[132] *Talmud Bav'li, Ta'anit* 31a

."[133] It was thus a dance of truth and authenticity, reminding us to celebrate beauty for its own sake, family upbringing or background for its own sake, and inner beauty for its own sake and not contingent on outer appearances – corresponding in turn to the three components of each our souls: נֶפֶשׁ *nefesh* = body soul manifestation (physical attraction); רוּחַ *ru'ach* = emotive soul manifestation (character, personality attraction), and נְשָׁמָה *neshamah* = supraconsciousness (transcendence, tantric, attraction to the other's soul-self but not to the neglect of the celebration of body and emotions). And what more opportune period to face these truths within ourselves and to have them mirrored back to us than on the Day of "Letting Go of Ego," or Yom Kippur?

This very aboriginal Jewish rite of dancing in the vineyards on Yom Kippur is deliberate. It is to teach us about forgiveness and about intimacy -- that both are empty if they lack joy, if they are not danced into aliveness in the vineyard, in the place of transformation and alchemy. Judaism therefore stresses the importance of rejoicing between intimate partners during this period[134] and the importance of joy in connecting to Creator.[135]

---

[133] *Talmud Bav'li, Eruvin* 65a
[134] Deuteronomy 24:5
[135] Deuteronomy 28:47; Psalms 100:2

It was in the vineyards that single women m.
themselves vulnerable to single men seeking mates.
you want me, the Feminine declared to the Masculine
you have to want my joy, my song, my dance. You have
to come find me in the vineyard, in the place where
wine is born, so that our intimacy will be *intoxicating*,
not just convenient.

Regardless of our sexual orientation or
preference – on the very holy day of Yom Kippur, our
feminine side dances and chants this lesson to our
masculine side, reuniting what often gets fragmented
within us, challenging us to stop our unbridled and
complacent flow and awaken us to the song of truth
and authenticity, available from our Earth via her gift
of alchemy in the grapevines. As King David put it
some 3000 years ago: "Truth will sprout forth from out
of the Earth."

Yom Kippur, the ancient rabbis remind us, is a
festival, a יום טוב *yom-tov*, or *yontiff* in Yiddish. It is a
celebration; it is not a time for morbidity or anxiety. We
do not fast to deprive ourselves; we fast in order to
respond to our oft-neglected souls, to enable her to rise
to the forefront of our awareness. At the same time, we
do not neglect the **physical** joy of Yom Kippur.

The ancient rabbis put it this way: Customarily,
when people are summoned to appear before a mortal

rt, they approach in unattractive clothes, disheveled ir, and a countenance of morbidity, in trepidation of he outcome of the pending judgment. Not so, however, when the days of Godly judgment begins [High Holydays], for the Jews then are clad in white and groom their hair, and they eat and drink and rejoice in the conviction that God will do wonders for them.[136]

Yes, you heard right: "eat and drink and rejoice." Wrote the 16th-century Kabbalist Rabbi Moshe Cordovero: "It is the way of all of Israel to rejoice on the eve of Yom Kippur and prepare a festive meal, and this is the practice."[137] Another reason for this practice, wrote the 16th-century Rabbi Yeshayahu ben Abraham, is that by celebrating on the **eve** of Yom Kippur, one demonstrates one's faith that one's sins will be forgiven on Yom Kippur itself.[138]

In the days of King Solomon, some 3,000 years ago, our ancestors totally forgot about the High Holydays one year. It happened right after they'd finished constructing the First Temple in Jerusalem. They partied so hard in celebration of their accomplishment that Yom Kippur came and went and no one noticed. When the people realized they'd been

---

[136] *Talmud Yerushalmi, Rosh Hashanah* 57b
[137] in *Avodat Yom HaKippurim*
[138] in *Mesechet Yoma, Perek Torah Ohr,* No. 4

partying on Yom Kippur, they fell into sadness and depression, when a Voice was heard from the heavens, declaring: "Go and eat your bread in joyfulness and drink your wine in good-heartedness, for your actions were acceptable to God"[139] – reassuring them that their failure to observe the high holydays was not lost on a God who considered it no less holy that they had gotten caught up in celebrating a good cause.

The teachings are clear. Yom Kippur is the heart of what we call "Days of Awe," not awe as in fear and trepidation, but awe as in "Awesome!!" We have to do more than parrot prayers and fast. We have to approach this sacred period with an attitude that reflects our deepest hopes, our most favored scenario for the year to come, and hopefully an attitude that is marinated in joy. In the end, the ancients taught, we will all dance in the vineyard of love and bliss, in a circle around God who will be pointing at each and every one of us regardless of our station, our achievement, or the lack thereof, acknowledging each our individual uniqueness.[140]

---

[139] *Midrash Bamidbar Rabbah* 17:2
[140] *Talmud Bav'li, Ta'anit* 31a

# 13

## Our *Lucky* Number

More than 3,400 years ago, Moses channeled the famous "Thirteen Attributes of Divine Compassion" - or *Shalosh Es'ray Mee'dot* שלש עשרה מדות -- while traversing the great Mountain of *Elo'heem* in the desert of Sinai.[141]

And they are, as follows:

| | | |
|---|---|---|
| יה | *yo hay* | Infinite Love and Mercy Transcendent; |
| וה | *wa hay* | Infinite Love and Mercy Immanent; |
| אל רחום | *el ra'hum* | God of Womb-Deep Compassion |
| וחנון | *w'ha'noon* | and Tender Grace; |
| ארך | *eh'rekh* | of Lengthy Patience, |
| אפים | *a'payeem* | of Forbearance |
| ורב חסד | *w'rav hessed* | and Great Love |
| ואמת | *w'ehmeht* | and Truth, |
| נוצר חסד | *no'tzer hessed* | inspiring Love in |
| לאלפים | *la'alafeem* | Abundance, |

---

[141] Exodus 34:6-7

| נושא עון | *no'sey ah'wo'n* | lifting Us Out of Guilt |
| ופשע | *wa' fesha* | and out of Erroneous Actions |
| וחטאה | *w'hata'ah* | and out of Wrong Choices |
| ונקה | *w'nahkey* | and Cleansing Us |

When we chant these 13 Divine qualities on Yom Kippur, we need to know that they are not a list of ways in which God is nice and forgiving. They are rather a very finite glimpse into the unfathomable depths of Divine Compassion.

As a number, **13** represents *beyond the norm*, beyond comprehension, beyond capacity of reckoning. It is the dashing and trashing of any attempts at absoluteness. For example, there were 12 sons born to Jacob and Leah, and Rachel, and Bilhah, and Zilpah -- thus 12 tribes. These correspond in turn with the four pathways of birthing the three manifestations of soul in body [4x3 = 12]. The four pathways -- known as פרדס *PaRDeS* -- are: *P'shat* פשט literal, *Remez* רמז cryptic, *D'rash* דרש explorative, and *So'd* סוד secretive. The three manifestations of soul in body are: נפש *nefesh* [physical], רוח *ru'ach* [emotive], and נשמה *ne'shamah* [cognitive]. Each of these ways in which the soul is embodied forges its realization along four pathways, four modes of engagement of any encounter or experience in any moment:

פliteral פשט
cryptic רמז
דרש explorative
secretive סוד

But there is also דנה Dee'nah, the **thirteenth** child of Jacob, born of Leah, the one daughter, the mystery that comes and challenges the absolute. She is not even included in Joseph's dream of the family bowing to him. She remains elusive, a mysterious shadow behind the veil of illusion, reminding us now and then that things are not always the way they are cracked up to be. For instance, there are 12 months corresponding to the 12 tribes. But there is a thirteenth "extra" month that comes along every few years and challenges the absoluteness of our attempt to reckon even something as predictable as Time itself. Applying the number 13 to the Attributes of Divine Compassion is thus another way of saying there are no absolute numbers one can attach to these attributes, because, again, they are unfathomable.

Therefore did the sages remind us that if we get all teary-eyed and penitent on Yom Kippur or other times because we are afraid of God's wrath, our penance is pitiful and moot, and we are then more in need of God's healing than God's forgiveness. Rather, the quality of any decision to change our ways for the better depends on whether we do so out of love, fear. And when we do so out of love, we ourselv bring healing, to ourselves and to others, even to the world![142] Therefore, taught the second-century Rabbi Meir, "If you will make confession of your sins on the **eve** of Yom Kippur, do so with the approach of dusk, with the fading-out of the day"[143] -- in other words, let it go, release it, don't *schlep* it with you **into** Yom Kippur itself; don't spoil the romantic mood of the moment.

On Yom Kippur, then, our hearts begin to melt (gulp), because God's hand moves to caress us "beneath our heads,"[144] a gesture of supporting us with all that we carry; a gesture of understanding that we sometimes make wrong choices amid all the stresses and challenges in our lives.

So, you ask, with all this hullabaloo about love and romance and dancing in vineyards, why is the practice **not** make love on Yom Kippur!? Well -- because on this day "the Light of Mother of Above joins with the Light of Mother of Below."[145] Like the spontaneous merging of two flames into one, the

---

[142] *Talmud Bav'li, Yo'ma* 86a; *Sif'rey MaHaRaL, Netivot Olam*, Vol. 2: *Netiv Ha'Teshuvah*, Chapter 2, folio 152

[143] *Talmud Bav'li, Yo'ma* 87b

[144] Solomon's Song of Songs 2:6

[145] Zohar Vol 3, folio 102a

ne of the Beyond meets in intimacy, joins with, the ame of the Immanent, Heaven with Earth, the Infinite with the Finite, Mother of Above, who is called "Friend," with Mother of Below, who is called "Bride," and also "Sister," for the earth, wrote Abraham Joshua Heschel, is our sister.[146]

> Mother of the Above Realms, she is called Friend, because of the love of God that flows through her and which streams unceasingly to all the universes. Mother of the Below Realms, she is called Bride, and also Sister, for she is inseparable and intimately connected to all.[147]

**This** is why it is customary to not have sex on Yom Kippur – specifically between a man and a woman. "Because on that day, the Bride [Earth] receives Mother of the Above, and thus the [Creator] does not approach her in intimacy on that day."[148]

So, no wonder there was no Wrath of God stuff in response to our ancestors' forgetting to observe Yom Kippur while celebrating the completion of the Temple, the housing of the Holy of Holies, the very

---

[146] *God in Search of Man*, p. 92

[147] Sefer Ha'Zohar, Vol. 3, folios 77b–78a

[148] 16th-century Rabbi Yeshayahu ben Abraham [*Sh'lah*] in *Perek Torah Ohr* on *Mesechet Yoma*, No. 7; see also 16th-century Rabbi Moshe Cordovero in *Pardes Rimonim, Sha'ar Ma'hut V'Ha'han'hagah*, end of Ch. 21

**bed**chamber, so to speak, of the union of Create
Creation. And no wonder Yom Kippur begins w
we down here say so, because after all the initiatic
the arousal of Above, begins right here below.[149]

And no wonder the ancients believed that Yom
Kippur was the time when God created **Light** (passion),
and **Mountains** (earth reaching toward sky), and **Sky**
(sky reacting to earth's gesture with rain that then
impregnates the earth [Genesis 2:6]), and **Earth** (earth
births forth vegetation in response to sky).[150]

And no wonder the rites of Yom Kippur in
ancient Israel included women dancing in the
vineyards. Wine *evokes* passion. Dancing *stirs* passion.
Earth is feminine. And so they stirred and whirled and
rejoiced to inspire the union of Mother of the Above
with Mother of the Below. The men, however, did not
join with them. They were only allowed to observe.
This was not the time for men to join with women.
This was Woman's Time, and exclusively so. It was the
time of the two Mothers to join with one another in
intimacy, Earth Mother and the Heavenly Mother. And
the masculine attribute of God, the Chief of Heaven,
had to withdraw and hang with the guys outside the
boundaries of the vineyard where the feminine danced

---

[149] Zohar, Vol. 1, folios 29b, 35a, and 46a-b
[150] *Midrash B'reisheet Rabbah* 3:8

...lf into ecstasy. Rather, it was the men's role to ...d the space, to contain. It was actually a role-reversal: whereas women gift men with containment, tempering and directing their energies, on Yom Kippur the **men** took on this role while the women let go and danced uninhibitedly in the vineyards.

What more powerful way, symbolically and practically, of purging the altar upon which we layer our life struggles, our personal transformations. What more potent rituals of restoring our connectedness to Spirit. And so we pray on this Sabbath of all Sabbaths,[151] as we do on **every** Sabbath: "Restore anew our days, as they were in ancient times."[152]

The Yom Kippur rites described in the Torah were then a symbolic re-enactment of these dynamics, of the kiss of heaven and earth, of the restoration of the primeval relationship of Creator with Creation, beginning with the seclusion of the High Priest (the solitude of God before engaging in Creation), continuing with the offering of the Sacred Fire (God creating something from out of nothing by way of the implosion of the primeval Light, or energy), moving into the covering of the altar with the life force of specific species of animals, each representing a

---

[151] Leviticus 16:31
[152] Lamentations 5:21

particular quality of soul manifestation movin toward personal evolution, and preparing us for Great Love-In. This is the underlying intent of Yo Kippur. It is the annual erotic union of Creator with Creation, the blending of the Light of the Spirit Realm with the Light of the Physical Realm, the kiss of the two universes, of the hidden universe and the unfolding universe, of the known world and the unknown world.

# "And Noah Opened
the Window of the Ark"[153]

> "And Noah opened the window of the ark that
> he had built" – this is Yom Kippur, for the ark
> of Noah, she is Great Mother, and the window
> of the ark is the Central Column through which
> the light of the Torah, the hidden light, is
> illuminated.[154]

Noah opening the window of the ark was a daring act of faith in new possibilities against the tragic reality of a collapsed world. It was God who had **shut** the ark, as we read in Genesis 7:16; and now it was Noah who was opening it. The act of opening that window was an act of Creation re-engaging Creator. The "central column" through which the life force of the universe filters from the Realm of Spirit to the Realm of Matter -- from Light to Manifestation -- is represented in the ray of light that shone in through that window once Noah dared to open it, to open what God had shut; to move beyond resignation toward hope; to allow the Light of Genesis to restore a World of Nemesis. The act of opening that window was an act of romancing Mother of the Above. "For the ark of Noah, she is Mother of the Above" – she is what carries us

---

153 Genesis 8:6
154 *Tikkuney Zohar, Tikkun* 39, folio 79b, or 22a

across the chasm between what once was and what would hope **can** be, lifting us high above the Grea Flood of the abyss and carrying us patiently until we can muster enough strength and stamina and courage to open the window and allow the "hidden light," the Light of Genesis, to shine through and foster Newness in our lives.

But if the ark represents Mother of the Above, and the window the central column of Divine Light, then it would be more accurate to picture the Divine Light not as coming into the ark through the window but – on the contrary – emerging from **in**side the ark, **in**side of Mother of the Above, and illuminating outward **beyond** the ark! And so indeed it was. What we do here in the Below Realm, in the realm of the Created, activates, empowers, or disempowers the potency of the Divine Light that is willed from Above to Below, from Creator to Creation. At the window we **meet**, but only if we remove the covering and come out of hiding, out of resignation. It is only then that the union happens between the worlds.

An analogy to this is how one can be a good parent or relationship partner in terms of being present but not **really** present. Sure, you pay the mortgage or the rent, foot the utility bills, work hard for the upkeep, buy Birthday cards, Anniversary cards, Hanukkah esents, flowers, mouth "I love you," and so on. Or, you can do all of that, or even significantly less, but be actively, conscientiously, **deliberately** present, stepping out of **your** convenient Self space to engage the Other in **theirs**. In that moment, your flame reaches far enough toward theirs that both join to become as one. Likewise, God is here **all** the time, hanging out with the remote, keeping the sun, earth and moon in perfectly balanced orbit, getting it to rain now and then, making sure leaves are green, cacti have needles, and ravens have what to eat. You want more connection than that? So, again: What we do here in the Below Realm, in the realm of the Created, activates, waxes or wanes the potency of the presence of the Divine Light that is willed from Above to Below, from Creator to Creation.

# Dumping Trash at the Palace

On Yom Kippur, The One Who Spoke and the World Came into Being gets exceedingly high on joy over having gifted us with this special day. It is analogous to a king who discovers that his household and his servants are dumping their garbage at the gates of his palace. When he goes out to examine the garbage, he rejoices with a great joy. Likewise with the Holy Blessed One, who rejoices with a great joy for having gifted us Yom Kippur out of magnanimous love [even as we dump our sins at the gates of the Palace]. Not only that, but in the very moment when the Holy Blessed One examines our individual sins and forgives them, the Holy Blessed One does not become sad or disappointed but rather exults in great celebration and declares to the mountains and the hills, and to the valleys and the wadis: "Come join with me in celebrating this great joy around my having forgiven these sins."[155]

Humbug, you say. Just an isolated teaching.

Not really. Here is another one:

"They asked Wisdom, 'The consequence of the sinner, what is it?' Replied Wisdom, 'Those who sin shall be pursued by evil' (Proverbs

---

[155] *Midrash Tana D'bei Eliyahu Rabbah* 1:6

13:21). They asked Prophecy, 'The consequence of the sinner, what is it?' Replied Prophecy, 'The soul that sins is headed toward death' (Ezekiel 18:4). They asked Torah, 'The consequence of the sinner, what is it?' Replied Torah, 'Let them bring an offering and be atoned' (Leviticus 1:4). They asked God, 'The consequence of the sinner, what is it?' Replied God, 'Let them turn around and be forgiven', as is written (Psalms 28:8), 'God redirects the wayward onto the correct path.'"[156]

The message many of us seem to get around this taboo term we refer to as "sin" is that it "separates us from God." And that repentance – or in Hebrew תְּשׁוּבָה *teshuvah*, literally: Returning – is the act of narrowing that separation and reconnecting with God by acknowledging what we did wrong and working at not doing it again. However, the 18th-century mystic, Rabbi Tzadok Ha'Kohayn, gifted us with a deeper understanding of all this. He taught that actually you never left home. You did not create any separation of so much as a fraction of a *mili*-milimeter of distance between you and God when you made your *oops*. On the contrary, your capacity to make that *boo-boo* to begin with – not the wrongful act itself but the **capacity** to do it -- was made possible by God who breathes life into your being every moment.

---

[156] *Midrash Pesikta D'Rav Kahana, Shuvah*, para. 8

*Teshuvah*, according to Rabbi Tzadok, is  ̶ not a long arduous journey over some unfathoma ̶ deep chasm across a flimsy swinging rope bridge.  ̶ is the act of turning around to re-engage the One who has been behind you all along, even in the moment when you erred. It is hearing God saying, "Wait! Don't run away! Just turn around. I am right here!" It is the act of realigning your actions to where God would most likely have preferred it to be in the very moment that the breath of life was gifted to you **while** you were erring.[157]

And if we're too embarrassed to turn around, God accepts partial responsibility and says to us: "Okay, then, I will take the first step," as is written,[158] "Thus says *Hawayah*, 'Behold! I am returning....'"[159]

Bottom line, it is **we** who make God out to be some kind of exacting, judgmental ogre. Like God said in an interview set up by the prophet Jeremiah: "Is it **me** that they anger? Is it not their own guilt that they are projecting on me?"[160]

The God of Love is not an alien concept to Judaism except in the minds of those bent on

[157] *Tzid'kat Ha'Tzadik*, No. 100
[158] Jeremiah 30:18
[159] *Midrash Pesikta Rabbati, Shuvah Yisra'el*, folio 184
[160] Jeremiah 7:19

rediting it. As the Zohar puts it: "The highest of the heavenly realms is the Realm of Love. And therein does the Holy Blessed One dwell, for the Holy Blessed One is always enrobed in Love. And the Holy Blessed One does not ever separate Itself from Love. As is written: 'And a river flows forth from Eden.'[161] Indeed, it flows forth continuously, and bonds with the universe in Love."[162]

After all, what exactly does כִּפּוּר *Kippur* mean? Etymologically, it means to erase, to wipe away, to cleanse, to cover-over, to layer. As in Exodus 29:36 where translators have it as "and you shall **purge** the altar." But **how** does one purge the altar? By layering it, covering it over with the offerings. The more correct translation, then, is "you shall *cover* the altar," cleanse the altar by layering it, as in preparing the bed for intimate union, for the joining heaven and earth. Because, by our active involvement in preparing the bed, so to speak, we restore passions lost, we stir-up love gone rancid. The altar, after all, is the site of the union of spirit and matter, of Creator and Creation: "אֲתַר דִּי בֵיהּ יֶחְדּוּן רוּחִין וְנַפְשִׁין" – the site by which spirits and personas are unified."[163]

---

[161] Genesis 2:10
[162] Zohar, Vol. 5, folio 267b
[163] 14th-century Kabbalist Rabbi Shlomo Alkabetz, *Shabbat Zemirot, Yah Ree'bon O'lam*

How do we effect change in our lives? How we correct ourselves, improve ourselves? By **layerin** our patterns, our old not-so-wonderful habits with newer and **better** ones. Personal transformation, the Torah is teaching us, is not achieved by beating our chests in remorse alone, or by brooding over past mistakes. Rather, it is achieved by moving **forward**, layering it over with fresh ways of being, new and improved ways of conducting ourselves, **terracing** rather than excavating. Like David put it some 3,000 years ago: "Flee from bad, and do good"[164] – meaning, let go of the mistakes and layer them over with positive action instead of wasting a lot of time excessively uprooting and un-doing to the neglect of actually planting anew, of making some real-time changes.

---

[164] Psalms 34:15 and 37:27

# Altar of Alchemy

It then follows that the underlying purpose of the offerings on Yom Kippur was to transform judgment into mercy. The color of judgment was considered to be red, the color of mercy white. Fasting, for example, turns our bodily color from red to pale, white. This is also why we dress primarily in white on this holyday. The offerings, too, symbolized this very dramatically. The shaman, or כֹּהֵן *kohain,* sprinkled the altar with blood, with redness. The smoke that ascended toward the heavens from the sacrifice, from the bloody-red altar, turned white, thus transforming the attribute of judgment to one of mercy.[165] This transformation was done through fire, as fire represents (1) divine light, and (2) passion that burns within us, and which therefore leads us to choices that are right or wrong. So whatever choices we made that were wrong, that were the result of the misuse of our passions, of our divine fire, needs to be transformed homeopathically through that very same element, Fire. At the same time, the primeval Fire of Creation, of Genesis, birthed forth Divine Light,[166] as we mentioned earlier, and so the transformative, alchemical fire on the altar of Yom Kippur also reminds us that our capacity for

---

[165] Zohar, Vol. 2, folio 20b

[166] *Midrash Sh'mo't Rabbah* 15:22

transformation is made possible by the Divine Lig
that dwells within us always, even in the moments c
our wrong choices. Mother Fire is always keeping her
fires going for you, 24/7.

This process of turning red into white is also an
alchemical process of turning fire into water. The
color of the north in our shamanic tradition is red, and
the element keeper of the north is fire. The color of the
south is white, and the element keeper of the south is
water. The season of north is winter, the season of
south is summer. North is mystery, south is clarity. We
want to move from mystery to clarity, from fire to
water, from burning passion to calming waters, from
the hiddenness of winter to the blossomness of summer.
From red to white. Therefore, the bullock which the
*kohain* sacrificed on Yom Kippur was positioned
facing in the direction of south.[167] So **during** Yom
Kippur we poured **blood** over the altar, and **after** Yom
Kippur, on the ensuing festival of סֻכֹּת *Sukkot*, we
poured **water** over the altar.[168]

This ritual of transformation, of moving from
judgment to mercy, is further symbolized in the rites
of the sin-offering in general. It was the role of the
*kohain* to welcome the sinner to the altar place with a

---

[167] *Talmud Yerushalmi, Yoma* 17b
[168] *Mishnah Sukkot* 4:1 and 9

untenance of joy, and to turn the tone of the sinner's confession from one of morbidity to one of celebration. And it was the Levite's role to offer song and music to gladden the heart of the one who came with his or her sin offering,[169] as is written in Psalms 100:2 -- "Serve *Hawayah* with joy; come before [*Hawayah*] in song." It is therefore that the offerings are always mentioned as קָרְבָּן לַיָ־הֶ־וָ־ה *korban l'yhwh*, rather than קָרְבָּן לְאֱלֹהִים *korban l'eloheem*, "an offering to *Hawayah*," rather than "an offering to *Elo'heem*." יְ־הֹ־וָ־ה is the God-Name that carries the attribute of mercy. אֱלֹהִים is the God-Name that carries the attribute of judgment. The rites of the sacrifice is directed to *yhwh* so that judgment – or *Eloheem* -- will blend with, transform into, morph into: mercy, into the quality of *yhwh*. As is written in that same psalm: "Know that *Hawayah* **is** *Eloheem*."[170]

---

[169] Zohar, vol. 3, folios 8a-b
[170] Psalms 100:3

# The Great Cringe:
# Forbidden Sex

What about the laws of sexual immorality that are customarily read about in the Torah portion which the ancient rabbis selected for Yom Kippur? And why on Yom Kippur, supposedly the day of the great **love**-in? Well, that is exactly **why** we read about these prohibitions, because in the era when these no-no's were first instituted, the world around us was brimming with religious worship rites that involved people using people sexually under the guise of worship. These are then specific prohibitions having to do with ancient cultic rites of incest and sodomy as religious ritual, as distorted attempts (from our perspective) at connecting with the Divine – rituals that we were not to emulate, that we were not to learn from amid some of the cultures surrounding us at the time.[171] Our rituals were not to be about abusing ourselves or others in order to placate or influence a higher power. Our rituals were about transformation, within and without, and within the context of faith in a deity who is not exacting, not foaming at the mouth, not demanding of bribes, and who waits for us to take the first step in engagement through rites that empower us, gladden us, and transform us. And so we read about what *not* to do,

---

[171] Leviticus 18:3 and 24-30 and 20:23

how *not* to serve God,[172] how *not* to expiate our wrongs, contrasting with the ways in which some of the other cultures in our vicinity did it back in those days. Our way is by joyful celebration and meaningful rites that raised us high, not brought us down, and certainly not at the expense of others.

These ritualistic abominations of some of the cultures around us represented to us the magnanimous human error in presuming that Creator is hidden from Creation and must be conjured into response and reaction by means of orgiastic rites. Judaism taught the direct opposite, that Creator dwells within Creation, breathing the Life Breath of existence into the nostrils of all beings across each and every moment. And that, on the contrary, any conduct that smacked of abuse, of people using people for their own sexual gratification in the name of religion while claiming it to be the will of God, was outright despicable.

It is then a serious misnomer that Judaism intended to de-feminize spirituality, and that all of the old so-called Goddess religions of Cana'an and vicinity were sweet and innocent and flourished peacefully before the Jews came along and disrupted them. Judaism forbade only those religious practices that took life for granted, that practiced child sacrifice,

---

172 Deuteronomy 12:31

virgin sacrifice, etc., as actually discovered in archeological digs of ancient Canaanite sites.[173] On the contrary, Judaism did more than most other ancient cultures to lift woman up to the status of equality in civil rights and spiritual recognition. "Ancient Israelite women," concluded one feminist scholar back in the roaring seventies, "fared better than modern western women."[174]

Yom Kippur is indeed the Day of the Great Love-In, and Judaism has always celebrated the sensuous no less than it has celebrated life itself and all of its wonder. At the same time, our ancients cautioned us that the overwhelming can easily overwhelm us to overwhelm others. And so, on Yom Kippur we engage the sensuous *tantrically*, so that we might stroll into the new cycle of time from a place of sanctified honor and balance rather than from a place of rationalized disregard and desperation.

---

[173] Nigel Davies, *The Human Sacrifice* [William Morrow], p. 51; Donald Harden, *The Phoenicians* [Prager, Inc.], p. 95; James Frazer, The Golden Bough [MacMillan], p. 327

[174] Rosemary Radford Ruether, *Religion and Sexism: Images of Woman in the Jewish and Christian Traditions*, by [Simon & Schuster], p. 70).

# SUKKOT

## Festival of the Lean-To

**Mother Water shows up most prominently on Sukkot**, as this festival is very much about praying for good rains in the coming winter moons. In fact – as mentioned earlier -- in ancient times, while we always poured wine over the altar, on Sukkot we poured water.[175] Water cleanses us of all that guilt or negativity we might have inadvertently drudged up during Rosh Hashanah. We are not to take this with us into the new year cycle. Rather, we call upon the waters of sky and earth to wash it all away, as is written:

"And I will pour upon you waters of clearing, and you will be cleared of all your overwhelmingness, and from all of your foibles will I clear you."[176]

*Sukkot* is about fluidity, softening all of the intensity that sometimes overrides the more joyful aspects of the High Holydays, too often ritualized in

---

[175] *Mishnah Sukkot* 4:1 and 9
[176] Ezekiel 36:25

solemnity when they are anything but solemn, as we learned in the previous pages. They were days of celebration, prayer, hope, faith, dance, song and chant. And if it didn't quite happen that way for you, there was always *Sukkot*: "Anyone who has not witnessed the celebration [on *Sukkot*] of the Drawing-Out of the Waters, has not witnessed true joy in their life."[177]

Having called to the forefront our past wrongdoings through the introspective rituals of Yom Kippur, we would be inclined to follow this high holyday with judgment, as in **self**-judgment, instead of actually letting **go** of our past wrongs and moving **on**. We were therefore given the post-high-holyday ritual of *Sukkot*, literally: "Shelters," or "Lean-To's," where our past wrongs become the very shade, the very protective shields from the fires of judgment, and become symbolic of Divine Compassion overriding Divine Judgment. And as our ancestor Jacob built *sukkot* to shelter his animals,[178] we too do so to embrace our impulsive animal qualities with compassion and remove our judgment of those qualities within ourselves even though we can easily attribute to them most of our past wrong-doings.[179]

---

[177] *Mishnah, Sukkah* 5:1
[178] Genesis 33:17
[179] *Sefer HaShl'lah, Mesechet Sukkah, Ner Mitzvah*, Chapter 46

*Sukkot* is the final phase of the rites of our harvest season -- Rosh Hashanah and Yom Kippur having been the first two, during which we gleaned from our fields and from our insides what is good, and dispatched to the compost pile what is not so good. It is the actual harvest gathering time, and we have in our homes more bounty from the harvesting than we had all year round. It is a gluttonous time, as our tables are then filled with wide varieties of produce we have gathered from the earth and her trees.

And just then, precisely when we feel all this wealth of bounty, we are instructed to take these riches outside of the comfort of our solid, permanent-structured homes, and have a meal of it in a flimsy temporary lean-two with an even less-dependable roof comprised of disconnected branches and leaves. It is a lesson in humility and a dramatic reminder of exactly where our bounty actually comes from.[180] Just when we are inclined to feel swell-headed over our having accomplished all this personal growth through our hard work in both the planting and picking seasons, we are gently humbled -- lest we declare "My power, and the might of my hand has achieved all this";[181] lest we forget where the flux of our blessings originates.

---

[180] *Menorat HaMa'or*, Vol. 3, Part 4, Ch. 1
[181] Deuteronomy 8:17

And so there we sit, singing, celebrating, welcoming the spirits of the ancestors each of the seven nights of *Sukkot*, vulnerable to the elements, unprotected, unsheltered, aware of how truly fragile we are at all times, and how the goodness of Creator sustains us even in those myriad moments when we are unaware of the miracles of our existence; even during the many moments we take life for granted.

But there is more to this festival.

The early masters of the Kabbalah reminded us that the Torah's first mention of the word *Sukkot* (literally: temporary shelters) appears not at all in regard to the festival we know by that name, but in the story of our ancestor Jacob. The Torah recounts how – following his reconciliation with his brother Esau -- he constructed "*Sukkot*" – temporary shelters -- for his herds: "And he made *Sukkot* for his flock, and therefore they called the name of the place *Sukkot*."[182] The second mention of *Sukkot* in the Torah is in reference to the first site to which Moses led our people during their exodus from Egypt: "And the Children of Israel journeyed from Ramses and headed for *Sukkot*,"[183] as in a place called "*Sukkot*."

The celebration of *Sukkot*, we are taught, is a

---

[182] Genesis 33:17
[183] Exodus 12:37

celebration of Great Mother, "for She is *Sukkah*, our shelter, our source of compassion against the forces of judgment, as She hovers over us as a mother protects her children."[184] Therefore must the shade of the *sukkah* roof-cover be greater than the sunlight, taught the 16th-century Rabbi Yeshayahu ben Avraham, for the sunlight is representative of the consuming fire of judgment, and the shade is representative of the sheltering compassion that Great Mother shadows over us. Not even the walls of the *sukkah* qualify as shade, he wrote, as walls are too much associated with judgment, in that they confine and limit. Rather, the roof covering alone must provide more shade than sun. Therefore, he continues, was this festival given to us to celebrate almost immediately after Yom Kippur, after our sins have been forgiven, just as Jacob our ancestor built *Sukkot* for his flock immediately after he had reconciled and exchanged forgiveness with his brother Esau.[185] It is in **this** theme of *Sukkah* that we dwell in this ritual lean-to for seven days[186] -- the *Sukkah* of reconciliation, during which Great Mother hovers over us as she did during the seven cycles of Creation: "And the Spirit of *Eloheem*, She hovered over the primal Waters."[187] And as the second-century

---

[184] Zohar, Vol. 2, folio 186b and Vol. 3, folio 100b
[185] Genesis 33:4
[186] *Sefer HaSh'lah, Torah Ohr*, Ch. 3
[187] Genesis 1:2

Rabbi Leyvee reminded us, the seven sacred offerings we offered over the seven days of *Sukkot*, were on behalf of the surrounding nations of that period[188] -- even on behalf of those amongst them who were our sworn enemies -- in commemoration of Jacob's reconciliation with his estranged brother, Esau.

Another deep teaching, attributed to the 16th-century Rabbi Meir Gabbai of Istanbul, goes like this: "The mystery of *Sukkot* is nestled in a deeply concealed thought, out of reach of the highest-flying eagles, and unknowable to any who ask 'Where?' From this nest of wisdom emanates the rays of the light of the World to Come, those very rays of Divine Wisdom Light that once spiraled out of its primordial point of Genesis into the Six Directions of corporeal existence and merged with Bathsheba the mother of Solomon to become the Seven Days of *Sukkot*."[189]

Wha...? Bathsheba? Yes, the very same Bathsheba who lived 3,000 years ago and with whom David had his scandalous affair. She represents personal transformation, as she turned David's illicit affair with her into a sacred union from which Solomon was eventually born – Solomon, who embodied both divine wisdom and peace, and who then continued the

---

[188] *Talmud Bav'li, Sukkah* 55b
[189] *Sefer To'la'at Ya'akov*, folio 70

near-kinked lineage of the Messianic dream. Likewise, the disconnected branches and foliage with which we cover the roofs of our *Sukkot* represent the spoils of our harvest[190] and thus also the sins which we have let go of during the Rosh Hashanah/Yom Kippur period, disconnected from their roots – from us – and now transformed into sacred implements intended to shelter us from judgment, intended to represent the compassionate sheltering of Great Mother.

So, yes, there is more to *Sukkot* than sitting in a lean-to. There is more to it than the literal understanding of commemorating a time we dwelled in lean-to's in the desert. When God is quoted as saying, "For I caused the Children of Israel to dwell in *Sukkot*,"[191] it is not referring to lean-to's but to that special place, that sacred theme, corresponding to Jacob's *Sukkot* that he built for his animals, and for a sacred oasis called *Sukkot*, where God brought us to have some respite and comfort after 210 years of slavery and before leading us on a long and treacherous journey across the desert. There is a lot more to the festival of *Sukkot*, wrote the 16th-century Rabbi Yehudah Loew of Prague, "for the event of our having dwelled in *Sukkot* during our exodus journey is not the primary reason for celebrating *Sukkot*. It goes deeper

---

[190] *Menorat HaMa'or*, Vol. 3, Part 4, Ch. 1
[191] Leviticus 23:42

than that...."[192] And now you know some of the depths of that depth. But only some. There is a lot more where these came from.

During these seven days we are also supposed to be praying for good winds, good rains, and a healthy earth through the ancient ritual of holding a palm branch combined with willow and myrtle branches and a citrus fruit called an אתרוג *et'rog* and shaking this combo in all four directions, as well as to sky and earth, as is written in the Torah: "On the fifteenth day of the seventh month, when you have gathered in the yield of your land, you should celebrate a festival for Infinite One for seven days. And you should take the "fruit of the Tree of Splendor [הָדָר פְּרִי עֵץ]," the branch of a palm tree, along with branches of myrtle and branches of willows that grow by the stream, and you should rejoice before *Hawayah Elo'heem* for seven days.... You should settle into *sukkot* for seven days, so that future generations will know that I inspired the Children of Israel to settle in *sukkot* when I took them out of the Land of Egypt."[193]

But *really.* What is so significant about commemorating camping-out in a lean-two? After all, our ancestors actually rarely lived in these things and

---

[192] *Gevurot Hashem*, Ch. 48, folio 201
[193] Leviticus 23:39-43

are instead recorded throughout the Torah as living mostly in **tents** during their exodus from Egypt, not huts.[194] *Sukkot*, then, is more than huts. It is about stopping dead in our tracks and taking some time out to appreciate what happened. Quite often, we tend to move on too quickly following a sacred event, or a moment of being gifted something significant by someone. How much time do we take to sit back and appreciate what we have received, compared to how much time we invest in pushing onward? How much more do we expect of our loved ones, compared to how much we consciously appreciate what they have already done for us? Or how much they mean to us, as is? The moment our ancestors were liberated from Ramses-the-Second, they no doubt became entirely focused on the journey ahead. They no doubt asked, "Okay, what's **next** on the agenda?" -- rather than remain a few moments with the enormous gift of having been liberated from slavery. They were therefore instructed to settle in *sukkot*, and to construct *sukkot*, and to camp-out in *sukkot*, in these flimsy, temporary lean-twos, and take in what they had just received. Judaism refers to this as *hakarat ha'tov* literally: "recognition of the good." This is what *Sukkot* is also very much about: taking time to recognize the gifts in our lives, whether it be our health, our wealth,

---

[194] For example, Exodus 33:8 and 10, and Numbers 24:5

our partners, our children, our selves, and so on. It is a period during which we take stock of our harvest yield and spend some time **appreciating** the gift of it instead of rushing right out into the field again to plant more for **tomorrow**. As the ancient rabbis put it: "Before you pray for what you *want*, be thankful for what you already *have*."[195] Before we become annoyed at what others have not *yet* done for us, let us take some time out to be thankful for what they have *already* done for us. Before we throw up our arms in disgust over **un**answered prayers and **un**realized dreams let us take some time out to appreciate the prayers that *have* been answered, the dreams that *have* been realized.

But of course the question remains: Can we not acknowledge our life gifts in a house or a tent? Why a *sukkah*? Because, while we are encouraged to take time to recognize what we have received, we are not to tarry too long in that place either, to the point of enshrining it, which leads in turn to feeling like we owe, which in turn takes away the gift sense of the blessings in our lives and leaves us with an emotional IOU in its place. We are obliged to acknowledge, but not to owe. Therefore, we take the time to acknowledge what's been good, but we do so in a *temporary* dwelling. Even a tent won't do for this ritual since a

---

[195] *Talmud Bav'li, B'rachot* 30b

tent is a dwelling we pack up and re-use again. We don't want to be re-visiting our gifts same-old, same-old. Rather, we want to re-visit our gifts each yearly cycle anew, completely fresh, by reconstructing from scratch a whole new *sukkah*.

The four species of Sprouting Beings we employ during the rites of *Sukkot* remind us of the gifts of **balance** (the אתרוג *et'rog* fruit, which bears both the feminine and masculine qualities), **shelter** (the לולב *lu'lav*, a yet-unopened palm branch), **empowerment** (the הדסים *ha'dasim*, or myrtle branches, as myrtle endures long after it is uprooted, or without water), and **sustenance** (the ערבות *ara'vot*, or willow branches, which flourish only within water's reach). Holding these qualities in our hands, we wave them to the four winds and to the sky and to the earth, to create a sacred space around us, above us, below us. Within this space we can savor the gifts of yesterday by weaving a hedge around the moment, enabling us thereby to step into the uncertainty of tomorrow from a point of strength.

Now, this is private. Don't tell anybody, but when we arrived in the Land of Canaan after 210 years of slavery in Egypt and 40 arduous years of schlepping across the desert, we observed the ritual of *Sukkot* maybe just once, and maybe just to make Joshua happy.

But then we got so comfortable settling into our ancestral homeland that we ditched the lean-two part of it altogether and reveled in our newly-built more *permanent* adobe-style homes. After all, the long laborious desert journey was over. We'd come home. And anyway, since when did we actually dwell in flimsy *sukkah* huts while sojourning through the desert? Maybe once when God asked us to. But the rest of the time we pitched tents, right? Not *Sukkot*. Balaam didn't say "How goodly are thy *sukkah* huts, O Jacob" --- he said "thy tents"![196] Tents, tents, **tents**! So, eventually we got comfy, and stopped doing the lean-two part of *Sukkot*.

And then, 800 years **later**, many of us – especially our spiritual leaders and prophets -- got taken captive by the Babylonians and exiled. And seventy or so years after **that**, we came home again, thanks to the Persian warrior Cyrus.[197] And when we returned, we were so happy and relieved that we got back our land and our independence that one of the first things we did was build lean-to's on our roofs and in our yards, and celebrated *Sukkot* in actual *sukkah* huts for the first time in eight hundred years! As is written in the Book of Nehemyah – "And the community of captives that now returned built *sukkot*

---

[196] Numbers 24:5
[197] Ezra 1:1-8

and dwelled in the *sukkot,* for the Children of Israel had not done this from the days of Joshua until that very day; and there was great rejoicing."[198]

You have to read this with a keen eye. For example, Nechemyah is recounting how it was specifically those returning from *captivity* who built and dwelled in *sukkot,* not the rest of us who had remained in the homeland all along. It would seem that those of us who had not been carried away into exile continued to **not** observe that part of the festival having to do with *sukkah* huts -- only those traumatized by the exile. This becomes even more evident as we read the section **prior** to this one, where Nehemyah recounts how the returnees were depressed, saddened by how much they had missed-out in regard to the knowledge and practice of their tradition during their exile, and so much so that they wept when they realized it was Rosh Hashanah and when they heard the leaders read from the Torah scrolls about the rituals of Rosh Hashanah. The leaders then had to stop everything and console these folks, and assure them that Rosh Hashanah was a festive time and that they ought to – and I quote -- "go home and eat rich foods and drink sweet beverages and send gifts to the disadvantaged;

---

[198] Nehemiah 8:17

for today is holy onto our Master, so do not be sad, for the joy of God is the very source of your empowerment."[199]

Puzzling. Because, eventually it appears that **all** of the Jewish people re-adopted the particular rite of *Sukkot* having to do with constructing temporal huts and living in them for seven days. It seems that we empathized with our returning sisters and brothers and joined them in their zeal of renewing a ritual that had been shelved for some eight centuries. And lest you surmise that the returnees built *sukkah* huts and lived in them because they'd just gotten back and were otherwise homeless – obviously this was not so. Because Nehemyah describes them building these sheds "upon their **roofs** and in their **courtyards.**"[200] On another level, then, *Sukkot* also has something to do with trauma. It is facing the temporary and very fragile and unpredictable nature of life -- namely, that nothing is permanent. Nothing is absolute. Nothing is guaranteed. No promise, no plan, no vision. We exist in a precarious reality. We tried to deny this by dismissing that part of the *Sukkot* ritual having to do with facing just that, with facing the shaky, vulnerable nature of our existence. And so we lived happily ever after. Until the Babylonians descended upon us and pulled the rug of security and complacency from under

---

[199] Nehemiah 8:9-11
[200] Nehemiah 8:16

our feet. We were then so shaken, that when it was over, we realized immediately the gift inherent in the ritual of the flimsy *sukkah* hut. And we re-adopted it; **all** of us. And we observed that rite uninterruptedly for the ensuing 2,500 years – onto this very day. Its lesson became, among other lessons of our tradition, a significant factor of our uncanny survival through the length and breadth of the longest exile ever known for any one people in all of human history.

It is no wonder that the ancient rabbis correlated *Sukkot* with the ancestor Jacob. Jacob lived an unsettling life. He could never just really settle down without being uprooted the moment he leaned back in his favorite armchair. He was always on the move, always dealing with one challenge or another. When we celebrate *Sukkot*, we remember that this flimsy lean-to we sit in is closer to the reality of our life walk than the solid house or apartment or condo we live in during the rest of the year. And more than that, it is more reliable by virtue of its fragile, temporary nature. After all, the numerical value, or גְמַטְרִיָא *Gemmatria*, of the word סוכה *sukkah* is **91**, the same *Gemmatria* for the Hebrew word צא *tzay*, which means "leave." On *Sukkot* we leave the comforts of our illusion and enter the realm of our reality. It is therefore ironic that while the Torah implores us to rejoice in our celebrations of the festivals -- "And you shall rejoice!"[201] -- *Sukkot,* however, is the only festival for which the Torah adds: "And you shall be **VERY** happy!"[202]

That is the challenge. Can we find joy in our temporariness? In our vulnerability? In our fragility? In the uncertain? In the unpredictable? In the precarious nature of our times? Can we sit and eat in a shaky hut exposed to the elements and sing like we've never sang before? That is the mystique of the Jew. That is our strength, our history, our heritage, our model for all.

And that is **truly** living in the consciousness of the Spiral of the Three Mothers who dance in the sacred space of mystery between Great Mother and Sister Earth.

---

[201] Deuteronomy 12:18; 14:26; 16:14; 26:11; 27:7
[202] Deuteronomy 16:15

# About the Authors

**Rabbi Miriam Ashina Maron, PhD, MA, BSN, RN,** holds a doctorate in Kabbalistic Healing and is an erudite scholar, author and teacher of ancient Judaic Mystery Wisdom. Her academic background and her experience in in-patient and out-patient psychiatric as well as medical-surgical units, combined with her immersion in pragmatic Judaic life wisdom, has helped her clients bridge their internal islands of body, mind and spirit toward more holistic resolution of biopsychosocial health and relationship issues. Dr. Maron's teachings, ceremonies, music, and entrancing movement practices, have captivated and moved the hearts of participants of all ages and cultural backgrounds across the U.S., Canada, Central America, Europe, and Israel. A prolific singer/songwriter as well, she has nine albums to her credit, which can be sampled at www.MiriamsCyberWell.com or *i-tunes.* Her book, *Ancient Moon Wisdom*, encapsulates her decades of research and teachings on Judaism's rich treasury of wisdom around the lunar cycles and their relationship to Hebraic tribal totems. She is also the co-author of *The Invitation: Living A Meaningful Death -- Ancient Jewish Teachings on Death and Dying and their Lessons for Enriching and Deepening the Quality of Living.*

 **Rabbi Gershon Maron Winkler, PhD** is a widely recognized pioneer in the restoration of aboriginal Jewish Mystery Wisdom. Author of fifteen books on themes of Jewish lore, law, history and mystery, his refreshing teachings are harvested from more than four decades of immersion in ancient Judeo-Aramaic and Hebraic source texts and oral traditions. He is the author of *Magic of the Ordinary: Recovering the Shamanic in Judaism* and served many years as Hillel Director and Circuit-Riding Rabbi across the hills of West Virginia, as Spiritual Leader of Congregation Har Shalom in Missoula, Montana, as Forensic Hospital Chaplain for the State of Californioa, and as Guest Lecturer at numerous colleges, universities and communities across the U.S., Central America, Europe and Israel.

**For more information on programs offerings by the authors, visit:**

www.WalkingStick.org   www.MiriamsCyberWell.com
www.Patreon.com/FacesoftheSapphire

Printed in the United States
by Baker & Taylor Publisher Services